New Nations and Peoples

China

China

LOIS MITCHISON

with 108 illustrations and 4 maps

THAMES AND HUDSON

To Guy with much gratitude

© THAMES AND HUDSON LTD LONDON 1966
PRINTED IN GREAT BRITAIN BY JARROLD AND SONS LTD NORWICH

Contents

1   A New Nation?

CH'IN SHIH-HUANG-TI, so they say, built the Great Wall of China with men's bones as bricks and men's blood as mortar. His critics were boiled alive in a cauldron placed conveniently in one corner of his audience chamber. He burnt the Confucian books, and buried the Confucian scholars alive. His taxes, his conscription, his iconoclasm, and his cruelty made him the most hated man in China. For more than 2,000 years he was the classic example given to schoolboys of the strong wicked emperor.

However today Ch'in Shih-huang-ti is getting a new face. He was, in his way, 'progressive', the new Chinese leaders say. He fulfilled the needs of the China of his time. He was a unifier, and he suppressed 'corrupt elements' in his society. The Great Wall is 'a proud achievement of the Chinese working classes' even if they were 'somewhat exploited' in its making.

Ch'in Shih-huang-ti is not alone in the new light of respect accorded him. Since the break with the Soviet Union there has been a particular revival of interest in the 'strong' emperors of the past, and a new defence of the unique excellence of China's history. In their speeches and writings the older generation of communist leaders quote the classics of Chinese literature, philosophy and history. One of the first acts of the communists after they came to power was to re-furbish China's museums and historic buildings. Ancient Chinese culture and learning has once again become the serious study and a source of inspiration for the new generation. China's national claims to have done most things in the world first and better have been re-emphasized. Russian scholars recently quoted ironically the Chinese historians who believed that Confucius

7

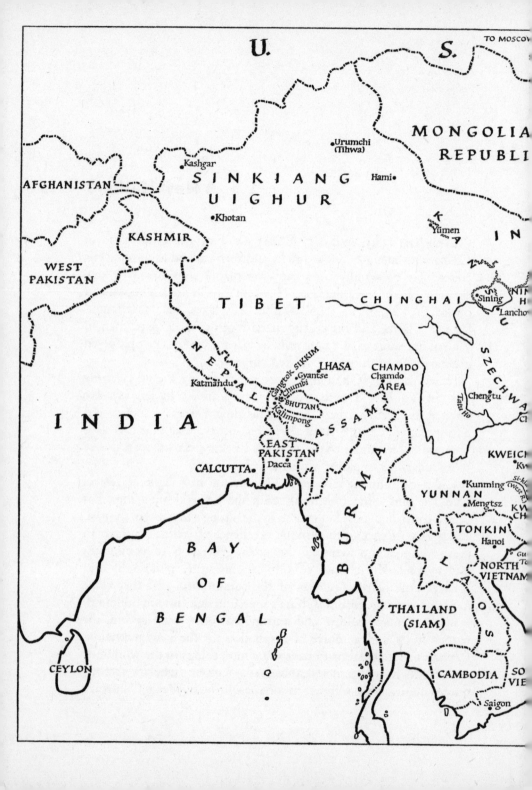

Political map of China

had been a formative influence on the French Encyclopaedists, and on the eighteenth- and nineteenth-century German philosophers; and that the even more remote and ancient *Book of Changes* inspired some of Liebnitz's mathematical ideas.

If their past continues to be so important to the Chinese, what claim has China to call herself a 'new nation'? Are the established traditions of over 3,000 years of civilized, centralized, government simply continuing into the present? In Chinese history good rulers have always emphasized the national heritage and the virtues of their predecessors. Is this what is happening now? The fourteenth-century novel, *The Three Kingdoms*, begins with the words: 'If the kingdom has long been divided, it must be united again; if it has been united, it must be divided again.' Were the years between the Nationalist revolution of 1911 and the establishment of the communists in 1949 only another of the classic periods of disorder? Civil war, foreign invasion, famine, and floods are as characteristic of all the historic interregnums as they were of the period between 1911 and 1949. By Chinese standards it was, if anything, a short interregnum, but perhaps the 50 years of decaying Chi'ng rule before 1911 should be counted with it. Then, like the strong emperors who ended disorder and founded new dynasties, Mao Tse-tung and the Communist Party have re-established internal order and morals, reformed the system of taxation, extended Chinese rule over rebellious frontier peoples, and put China back almost in her old place as the important nation, the central country, of the world. In return the Chinese people have given Mao the adulation due to the imperial Son of Heaven. Even the simplicity of his life, his insistence on the warts painted into his portraits, has good precedents behind it. This was how Liu Pang, the rough peasant bandit who founded the great Han dynasty, behaved 2,000 years ago.

The other communist leaders, austere, uncorrupt, and, within reason, efficient, have been compared to the Mandarins, the civil servants who governed the Chinese Empire from the time of the Han dynasty onwards. Communist education and their way of recruiting officials are close to the old methods, if Marxist set books are substituted for Confucian ones.

It is not an unflattering comparison, and it is often made by liberal well-wishers of the Chinese communists; but they themselves reject it utterly. The Confucian world was static, looked backwards. The Marxist world is dynamic, and looks forward. Mencius, Confucius' greatest disciple, said that those who work with their hands always support those who work with their heads. In communism those who work with their hands are in theory, if not in practice, the natural leaders of society. In Chinese communism, particularly, intellectuals and officials can only think rightly and govern rightly if, as well as working with their minds, they also work with their hands. Prime Ministers, pianists, and philosophers volunteer for their Sundays spent digging or earth-carrying on the latest dam or road project.

The communists are, they insist, New men in a New China. The old emperors and their servants were sometimes 'progressive' within the framework of their times; but because they were not Marxists they could not even know whether they were on the side of progress, and they were not and could not have been aiming at communism. To know that they are on the side of history, progress and virtue (although this last word is only implied, not used, by the present Chinese leaders, in contrast to their predecessors) is reserved for the communists; and because only they are communists, truly one with the people and the people's interests, only they are in sight of the final goal for China, the millennium of the communist society.

If historical comparisons have to be made the proper people to compare to communists are the leaders of the peasant revolts. The more recent the revolts were, the nearer in time to the appearance of communism, the closer the peasants could get to communist ideas. The most honoured historical figures in China today are the leaders of the Taipings and the Boxers, two of the great peasant rebellions of the nineteenth century.

In science, art, the technique of farming and crafts, much, the Chinese communists said, could be learnt from the Chinese past. But it was essential, in their view, to pick out the right bits of the past. The achievements of the 'oppressing' class, 'decadent' painting and poetry, as well as 'feudal' philosophy or history had nothing, particularly in the first years of the new government, to teach the newly re-born Chinese people. Later the régime could afford to relax a little. Even Mencius could be rehabilitated. But it is always easier and safer for the scholar to praise works of learning, or works of art, like the Buddhist sculptures, made by men of working-class origins, admired by the ordinary people, and, on the whole, despised by the gentry of the past. Chinese technology is politically popular: the inventions of the working class to make working-class daily life easier. Archaeology is popular too; and the articles in the foreign-language press describing the newly discovered Neolithic village houses did not fail to point out how fortunate the archaeologists were to be able to work on sites already partially dug to make the foundations of new towns and factories. (Neolithic village sites, about 7,000 years old, have recently been excavated over much of North and Central China. Chinese Neolithic villagers were particularly skilled potters, and among the most magnificent of their artefacts are the great painted burial urns of the Kansu sites.)

Under the communists, however, China's past could not outshine its future. Part of their pride was that what they did had no parallel in their country's history or even in the world's history. In particular, they claimed, the rural and urban communes and the way of life built round them were the beginning of actual communism, something never seen anywhere at any time before. There had been rule in China in the past that was comparatively good. Other countries, like the Soviet Union, were 'socialist', an improvement on capitalist. But only China had seen the dawn of absolutely good government. China, her leaders alleged, was new born; and, in her new birth, a model for all other new nations.

2   Colonizing China

SHEN NUNG, WHO WAS THE FOUNDER of the Hsia dynasty more than 4,000 years ago, was also a great farmer. He taught the Chinese, it is said, what crops to grow, when to sow, when to reap, how to clear the land, and how to ditch and drain. Among his successors was the Yellow Emperor, Huang Ti. At his court, so they say, men wrote on strips of bamboo, studied the stars, and made a calendar. The Yellow Emperor's wife, Lei-tsu discovered the silk culture; and in their joint reigns peace and virtue so abounded that a unicorn roamed the imperial park and a phoenix nested on the palace roof. The communists have restored the supposed site of Huang Ti's tomb in Shensi, and re-dedicated it to 'the father of the Han people . . .'.[1]

Some centuries before the first millennium B.C. the Hsias and their legends merge into the Shangs and known, written, and dated history. The Shang used inscribed bones to register the questions put to their state oracle and its decrees. The state, these writings describe, was ruled by priest kings who were buried in tombs of Egyptian splendour with their wives, servants, animals, and worldly possessions around them. It is from the excavation of these tombs that archaeologists have discovered the range of Shang skills. They inlaid bone with turquoise, carved jade and ivory, used musical instruments, and went to war in chariots. The serpentine Chinese dragon, longer and less massive than its European counterpart, and with a lion's head, makes its first appearance in the Shang carvings.

These Chinese contemporaries of Crete and later Mesopotamia and Egypt lived in one of the world's least comfortable cradles of civilization. The north Chinese climate is like Canada's. The summer is hot; but in the long cold winters temperatures drop to ten degrees below freezing for months at a time. There is a low rainfall of about 20 inches a year, fortunately most of it falling in the spring. The Hwang Ho (Yellow River), that flows through the rolling northern hills, and then out to sea over a broad coastal plain, floods or dries up frequently and unpredictably. One of the Hsia legends is of the Emperor Yu and the work he did when the Yellow River flooded in his time. He was, the legend says: 'eight years away from his home, and though he thrice passed the door he did not enter'.

In spite of the stories about the Emperor Yu the main Yellow River valley and the coastal plain was too great a challenge for the early Shang state. Just as Egyptian civilization began in the easier, if potentially less fertile, lands above the Nile Delta, so the Shang kings set up their first capital at Anyang in the loess hills to the northwest. These hills are more easily worked than the land near the river, and fertile enough to produce a wheat and millet surplus sufficiently large to support a court and cities. The loess dust of which they are made is unwooded (another advantage for early settlers who have, throughout world history, avoided forests). The villagers today, like their ancestors of Shang times, hollow themselves out cave homes and buildings, sometimes working under the cliffs, some- times burrowing under their own fields, so that no land is wasted. The only sign of a family can be smoke from a kitchen chimney blowing up through apparently deserted growing crops.

From these open grass-covered hills and the tributary valleys the early settlers gradually moved down to the main Yellow River valley, the coastal plain, and the further lowlands of North China. For thousands of miles there were no impediments to the pioneer farmers before they reached the mountains and deserts of the far west and north, the sea, and the forests of the Yangtze valley.

Unfortunately, to the north, the country was equally easy for nomadic horse-riders to move over. For centuries they raided the settled lands and towns, and retreated back to what was to be called Mongolia before the slow-moving foot-soldiers of the plain could close with them. In time along the northern frontier the settled farmers intermarried with the barbarians and learnt some of their war skills. It was from among these frontier people that the Chou dynasty came to overthrow the Shang in 1027 B.C. They fought with crossbows and elaborately carved short swords, and their first king claimed to have conquered because the last Shang ruler had 'despised the commands of heaven . . . was lazy and slothful, slighted the labours of government'.

The strength of the new Chou state, however, was quickly undermined by the independence of its nobles on their fiefs. From the ninth century until the final conquest of all settled China by Ch'in Shih-huang-ti in 221 B.C. the Chou Emperor kept only priestly power over what had by now become independent small states. Their rulers set up different systems of government, and there were constant wars between the states. Nevertheless, to the Chinese this is the classic period of their history.

The centuries of the decline of the Chou became to China much what ancient Greece was to later Europe. There were the same early heroic deeds and legends; and the same intellectual, political, and practical froth and experiment.

It cannot have been a comfortable period for a Chinese to live in. Plundering armies and unpleasant deaths were over-common. Yet, under the communists, just as it was before, it is the most often quoted period of Chinese history. At the end of the Chou, China, in all but details, is the country she remained for the next 2,000 years. The farms have become familiar. Hens, buffaloes, and wet rice cultivation had been introduced, probably from India or Burma. A late Chou text describes ploughshares, hoes, and scythes as farm tools. Houses and gardens are designed as they were to be for future centuries. Women wear gold, silver, and jade ornaments. Lacquer is used on furniture. Even chopsticks, the most character-istic of Chinese refinements, are first mentioned in the third century B.C.

Most of the ideas that have influenced the Chinese trace back to this period (and so do many more soon discarded by ordinary Chinese thinkers). It was the age of the philosophers. Confucius (Kung Fu-tzu – his name, like Mencius, was latinized by the

Jesuits), the most famous of them all, was born in 551 B.C., and spent much of his life travelling from state to state looking for a prince who would adopt his theories and found utopia. Later, Confucius' ideas were added to and tidied by Mencius during the period of '100 Schools of Philosophy'. (Typically Mencius included an arithmetically logical tax system.) The rulers of the time encouraged philosophers as ornaments to their courts and tutors to their sons and their nobles' families. As long as their views were not too outrageous, most of them said what they liked, and the ruler had no need to listen to them. Yang Shih, a cynic and an Epicurean, wondered 'if cosmically an idea is more important than the bowels', and preached that after death all men are equal in their 'rotten bones'.

The philosophers who had the most immediate influence on the rulers of the time were the Legalists.[2] They believed that man's nature was bad (a belief much less commonplace in China than in Europe) and could only be restrained by severe laws, rigidly enforced. Han Fei-tzu, the founder of the school, believed that major crime would be prevented if all minor crimes were, without exception, punished by death. In Legalist theory the state was supreme, its aim was conquest, and its ruler absolute.

The Lord Shang, a practical Legalist and one of the early advisers of the semi-barbarian state of Ch'in in the northwest, ordered that all trades and crafts should be suppressed as distractions from the main occupations of soldiering, farming, and weaving. Nobles who failed to distinguish themselves militarily were demoted; and the clothes, land, and servants allowed to those of different ranks were laid down in detail. The Lord Shang conquered the state of Wei, where he had been born, by asking the Wei prince to a parley and there taking him prisoner. In the end the Lord Shang was too much even for the Ch'in ruler who ordered him to be torn to pieces by chariots. (Typically – most of the Legalists came to unpleasant ends.) But the Ch'in state had started on its expansion over North China. The final conquest of the independent princes and the Chou overlord was completed in 221 B.C. by Ch'in Shih-huang-ti, advised by another Legalist, Li Ssu.

Li Ssu encouraged Ch'in Shih-huang-ti to massacre the 400,000 soldiers who had surrendered to him, and scatter the ashes of minor criminals in the streets of his capital. He and his imperial master broke the power of the great feudal families, and for the first time the emperor ruled through civil and military officers appointed by him to govern for a term of years.

The most famous of all the Ch'in achievements is the Great Wall: the mark of the northern boundary between China and the barbarian steppe. The wall stretched 2,000 miles east to west, over mountains and desert, rock and shifting sand dunes. It took Ch'in Shih-huang-ti 12 years to build, his best administrators and troops, and most of the resources of the newly united country. Heavy taxes were raised to pay for the wall, and anyone who crossed the emperor's pleasure was sent to labour on it. One of the most famous legends in China is about the princess from one of the newly conquered states whose husband was sent to work on the wall. He died, and she set out to find him. A spirit told her to cut her finger, hold it before her, and follow the trail of blood. It took her to her husband's body.[3]

Most of Ch'in Shih-huang-ti's wall was constructed by joining together and strengthening the older walls which had protected the small Chou states. Garrisons were stationed behind the wall, and there were defensive watchtowers every few hundred yards where archers could fight off horsemen's attacks.[4] After Ch'in Shih-huang-ti other emperors rebuilt and repaired the wall; and on the best known section near Peking today a troop of horsemen can ride abreast on the broad ramp between the side walls.

Part of Ch'in Shih-huang-ti's purpose when he built the wall was to end frequent barbarian raids on the plains people. Another aim, however, less generally acknowledged by his contemporaries and successors, was to keep the Chinese in as well as the barbarian out. The wall was built roughly along the line of the rising Mongolian plateau where rainfall becomes too scanty for intensive cultivation by hand on the orthodox Chinese model. Settlers beyond the wall needed bigger farms, animals and ploughs, not hoes. They were more thinly scattered than farmers in China proper, and more difficult to control and protect. They were also likely to ally with the barbarian and shelter politicalmal contents – generally an admini
strative problem for which there was no room in a tidy Legalist state.

The Great Wall was never particularly successful at keeping the barbarians out of China. Pushed back beyond the Wall the bar
barians built up their own political structure independently of the Chinese, and in times of dynastic weakness went round the Great Wall or through its less guarded points. (Its whole length was, naturally, seldom kept in repair.) Barbarian kingdoms set up in the northern plains after great slaughter and destruction were to punctuate Chinese history.

The Wall was, however, more successful as a boundary to Chinese settlement. There continued to be scattered farms beyond the Wall and strong emperors sent out military expeditions into the Steppe country. But the protection given the outlying settlers was sporadic, and the imperial court at most periods disapproved of them. Similarly the far-flung military expeditions were not the first step in the eventual Chinese colonization of new country, but sorties to show the Chinese flag, revenge raids, and enlist new allies.

The main tide of Chinese colonization set south and west, away from the danger of barbarian raids. This was approved of and encouraged by the imperial court. Ch'in Shih-huang-ti, like other strong emperors after him, needed settled new lands to feed his large army. In his search for them he sent a military expedition over the hills to the south of the Yellow River to conquer the Szechuan basin in the middle reaches of the Yangtze valley. Szechuan is one of the richest regions in China. In Ch'in Shih-huang-ti's day it was already irrigated, and had a large grain surplus.

Later Ch'in Shih-huang-ti sent expeditions over most of what is now China. Ch'in armies conquered the region around what was to be Canton, and moved into Vietnam. But the unification and settlement of the whole of China was not completed for another thousand years. From Peking to Canton, north to south through China, is farther than from Moscow to Paris. East-west, across the width of the country, it is 1,400 miles up the Yangtze from Shanghai to Chungking, and beyond Chungking there are hundreds of miles of mountains before the present western border. After the USSR and Canada China is the third largest country in the world.

In this continent of a country the main areas of modern settlement were to be the old northern centre of the Yellow River valley and its coastal plain; the Yangtze valley, particularly Szechuan and the delta of the river; and the West River valley and delta in the south, with the other surrounding valleys among the lower southern hills. These hills do not reach the coast on the southeast, and along the sea here there was more good arable land. The last settled farming area in China was the Yunnan plateau in the far southwest. Between these centres of farming and settlement there still are vast stretches of barren mountainous country. Less than a seventh of the Chinese countryside can be used for arable farming.

For more than a thousand years after the first Ch'in expeditions the imperial armies pushed their way over this inhospitable land. Little was known about the country and local tribespeople were often hostile. The south and the Yangtze valley was densely overgrown with forest, where tigers were the most feared wild beasts.[5] Most of the Chinese farmers who settled in the new country were soldiers from the armies. They married local women whose existing families were either killed or driven into the less fertile country. Sometimes tribal chiefs were given Chinese titles and offices, and they and their peoples, after a few generations, forgot their tribal origins. Sometimes the soldiers were backed by imperially encouraged migrants.

Farmers around Canton (now known as Kwangchow) still call themselves 'T'ang People' after the dynasty that arranged their settlement; and still speak, in the extreme south, a variant of the dialect common round Peking. A contemporary poet, at the time of this T'ang migration, wrote of the strangeness of the south:

'In the Southern Land many birds sing;
of towns and cities half are unwalled.
The country markets are thronged by wild tribes;
the mountain villages bear river-names.

Poisonous mists rise from the damp sands;
strange fires gleam through the night-rain.
And none passes but the lonely seeker of pearls
year by year on his way to the South Sea.'[6]

At the end of the thirteenth century Marco Polo described China as two lands. The north he called 'Cathay', and the south 'Manji'. Even now, although every inch of arable land in the south is settled, it is still a strange country to the northerner.

The very languages of the south are incomprehensible in the north. The same written language is used all over China. (One of the common sights of any city used to be the traveller writing out wants he could not talk about in an alien dialect.) And over the last decades schoolchildren throughout China have also been taught the Peking dialect whatever their mother tongue was. But in the south and far southwest, particularly, many farmers still cannot speak anything other than their local language. This may not be properly understood even in the next village. In the province of Fukien alone there are 108 different dialects. Cantonese itself is a lighter language with more tones in it than the Peking dialect. A particularly good language, Chinese say, for intrigue—political or amorous.

Southern village houses are built of straw and wattle rather than the bricks of the north. There is no need for the ovens and heated bedplaces which make the northern winter tolerable; and because the southern hills are better wooded than the north, wood, rather than dried dung, is used for fuel. The farmers grow rice, not wheat or millet, and, where the country and markets are suitable, tea, tropical fruits and vegetables. Farm animals and transport differ to the north and south of the Yangtze. In the north farmers use small donkeys and wheelbarrows; in the south men's (and women's) backs or buffaloes on the farms are used. In the southern cities the rich at one time were carried in sedan chairs.

The south is above all a different-looking country. Chinese landscape painters have seldom been interested in the flat, dusty northern plains where only the villages, and the groups of trees around surviving grave plots break the monotony of endless fields. Northern roads and village streets are wide and straight, so are the irrigation canals, and even the high dykes banking the much worked rivers of the plain. Some artists have drawn the Shantung hills of the northeast in their wild descent to the sea; but Shantung has a reputation as a dour province, something like the lowlands of Scotland, not given to the fine arts. Many more landscape painters have drawn the southern hills, the groves of bamboos there, and the terraced valleys. The most painted country of all is the curious karst landscape of the far south round Canton. Old limestone there has weathered into overhanging cliffs, caves, and the perpendicular, sugar-loaf type mountains which are characteristic of one sort of Chinese landscape picture. Southern streams, faster-flowing and more romantic than the great rivers of the north provide what the accepted masters of the classic painting taught was a necessary part of a balanced picture: wild country, rocks, water and trees.

As the armies and settlers pushing down from the north explored the country that was to be China, they were halted to the east by the Pacific Ocean, and to the west by the Himalayas, the other mountain ranges, and the deserts. In the northeast Korea, off and on, was a Chinese province; and there was trade with Japan. But beyond Japan the Pacific, for 2,000 years, was the end of the possible world. To the west, however, even the Himalayas could be crossed over the high passes, and for 1,500 years there was a limited exchange of ideas and trade with north India through the mountains. Tibet, off and on like Korea, acknowledged Chinese suzerainty.

North of the Himalayas better developed trade routes through the desert oases linked China to central Asia and the West. Some evidence suggests that 2,000 years ago the central Asian climate was wetter than it is now, the oases bigger, and the region more important. Through the oases China sold silk to the Roman Empire. The Roman economists worried about the export of Roman bullion to China to pay for this silk, and the Roman moralists thundered at the women who deserted honest, heavy homespun in favour of the soft transparencies from the 'Seres' (the Chinese: the silk makers – the only silk makers of the time). But the trade went on through intermediaries, and the two empires knew only rumours about each other.

However, it is in the south that Chinese border provinces merge most easily into what are now neighbouring states. North and central Vietnam were, for most of 2,000 years, governed as Chinese provinces. To the rest of Southeast Asia it is a short and relatively easy sea journey from South China. There is evidence of Han dynasty trade with Indonesia and Malaya in the second and first centuries B.C. There was probably some trade even earlier than that, from northern ports, before the south coast of China had been colonized by the Chinese.

At the beginning of our own millennium when the Sung dynasty were pushed south by the advancing Mongols, fleets were sent out to explore the southern seas. In 1178 Chou Ch'u-fei described the ships of the time as 'like houses. When their sails are spread they are like great clouds in the sky. Their rudders are several tens of feet long. A single ship carries several hundred men.' These ships carried Chinese ceramics as far as the east coast of Africa; and there was a well established sea trade with Ceylon, India, and Southeast Asia. The Indian rajahs particularly valued the Chinese green celadon plates because they believed the plates would change colour if poisoned food was put on them.

Under strong emperors, like Kublai Khan, part of the trade which came back to China was theoretically tribute from subordinate states. What came from China was then, again in theory, not equal trade but gifts to loyal subjects. Sometimes these claims to suzerainty were backed by governors, sent by the Chinese court, and naval or military expeditions; but how effective the empire was varied immensely from decade to decade. Sometimes even the pretence of tribute, although not the actual trading was dropped altogether.

Officially there was no Chinese settlement overseas. Special, and rarely given, imperial permission was needed for any Chinese to live outside China. But the groups of illegal settlers grew. Nearly all of them came from the four southern, and overcrowded provinces of Kwangtung, Kwangsi, Fukien, and Hainan Island. Chinese skill was valued in Southeast Asia and Chinese artisans settled in the major towns. After them came men to be local shopkeepers and to manage the internal trade of the south Asian countries; and in the nineteenth century some of the emigrants were farmers and unskilled labourers. There are now about 14 million Chinese settlers all over Southeast Asia. In most countries they are a sizeable and commercially important minority, and in the old Malaysia, with Singapore, there were more Chinese than indigenous Malay people.

As immigrants the disadvantage of the Chinese has been that they did not take the nationality of the country they settled in. Until the recent communist treaties, China did not acknowledge that a Chinese or the descendant of a male Chinese could ever stop being Chinese. Similarly territory that had once been Chinese was, in Chinese eyes, always Chinese. This means that Chinese maps and historians have always made very grand claims. There were recent shocked protests when Chinese communist maps showed parts of the Indian mountains and much of Southeast Asia as Chinese; but these maps could be paralleled by Ming, Sung and T'ang claims, and by maps published more recently by the Kuomintang. In the 1940s geography textbooks for Overseas Chinese schools marked most of Southeast Asia as Chinese provinces.

Nevertheless the Chinese do not think of these provinces as part of the Central Kingdom, China proper. To a Chinese 'his native place' is where he or his family originally came from. In Southeast Asia, and to some extent in the much later settlements in Manchuria and Sinkiang, the Chinese have taken a very British view of their empire. They live there temporarily, making their fortunes, and bringing 'the benefits of civilization' to the natives, and then they retire 'home'. A typical, pre-communist, emigrant pattern was for a young man to marry in his native village, leave his wife with his family, either pregnant or with a small baby (preferably, of course, a boy), and go to make his fortune overseas or in the empty northern lands. He might stay away ten, twenty or thirty years without his wife joining him, but he would send her and his family money. Ideally he returned with enough savings to buy a farm, support an honoured old age, and be buried in the family grave plots. In Chinese tradition it was a deplorable accident if the settler had to remain outside China; no other country could properly become his home, be a place where he could with full self respect leave his bones and establish his family worship.

3   The Order of Society

TO THE EDUCATED UPPER CLASS of eighteenth-century
Europe, particularly eighteenth-century England, Chinese Society
seemed almost wholly admirable. Chinese art, architecture, and
gardening were admired and copied. The state was orderly; far
better ordered than parts of Europe. The common people were
industrious and skilled. They were governed by an effective civil
service and a despot, all of them made benevolent (at any rate in
their professed sentiments) by their regard for the Confucian system
of law and learning.

'Li', propriety, the Chinese gentleman's control and balance,
was achieved through education and maturity. Its outward expres-
sions were good manners, a concern for the structure and formality
of human relations, and a desire to arrive at the right course of
action – the narrow path between two wrongs. As in eighteenth-
century England, over-enthusiasm and excessive piety were
condemned as suitable only for women and servants.

Yet it was a mistake, one made by many of the eighteenth-century
sinophiles, to see Confucius, the sage of this society, as a more
prominent, Chinese Lord Chesterfield. Confucius himself insisted
that he was a historian rather than a religious innovator or a meta-
physician. 'I have transmitted and do not create anew', he wrote in
the *Analects*. 'I am faithful to the men of old and love them.' (The
men of old were the god-kings of the Hsia and Chou dynasties and
their subjects.) By proper behaviour – the emperor and the officials
to the people, the people to their superiors and to each other – this
old Utopia could be re-created. It is a belief that the English and
French eighteenth century could parallel by reference to Greece and
Rome, or to the more primitive golden age discussed by Rousseau

among others. (Like the Chinese Rousseau believed that the conduct necessary to re-create this golden age would come 'naturally' to the properly educated.)

However, where the eighteenth-century view of this admirable, rational China went wrong was in forgetting that the Utopian Golden Age was partly magical. In their regulations about conduct, family, and state life, Confucius and his most influential follower, Mencius, included rites and sacrifices. Books on astrology, geomancy, and the appeasement of the gods were part of the Confucian classic (although most of them described traditions established long before Confucius' time); and these books became a respectable part of the examination syllabus of the scholar officials. By the standards of contemporary Europe, Chinese society of every rank was extremely superstitious.

It was an earthy sort of superstition. Chinese in a position to be moderately comfortable in this world were seldom concerned with the perils or rewards of the next. What was aimed at was the placating of forces which could make life uncomfortable in this world for those who accidentally crossed them; and the enlistment of magic on one's own side for one's own earthly advantage.

The most likely magical powers to do an injury to people were ghosts, demons, and dragons. Most villages boasted their own haunted places; and dragons, as well as broken dykes, were held responsible for floods. Moreover just as it was the official's duty to see that dykes were kept repaired, so he should placate local dragons by appropriate ceremonies. Proper rites were also needed to lay the evil ghosts of women who had died in childbirth, and the fox fairies who killed men with the importunity of their love-making.

Geomancy was the study of the proper placing of buildings so that the spirits of earth and heaven would be favourable to them. Geomancers were consulted during the nineteenth century, not only about the placing of tombs and palaces, but also about roads and military defences. It was better, orthodox Chinese officials considered, to have a gun ineffectively placed, than one that was militarily effective, but offensive to the spirit of the harbour it guarded. Geomancy was one of the most respectable of the magic sciences.

The proper balancing of earth forces – wind, direction, outlook, and soil – was closely allied to the ethical balances of propriety.

In the home magic and religious belief were more important to peasant families and to women than to men of rank. The most important of the minor deities of the household was the hearth god. He watched over the amity of family life and could be offended, not only by quarrelling, but also by such breaches of etiquette as a woman combing her hair in his sight. His paper image was burnt each year as part of the celebration of the greatest of the Chinese holidays, the New Year; and to sweeten the report he then made to heaven he had honey smeared on his mouth. In the village temples the gods charged with bringing rain could be recalled to their duties by being ducked, head first, into a pot of water. Similarly in times of too much rain the god's image would be left out overnight to appreciate for itself how much water there was about.

Much of the popular magic and rites in Chinese life came from Taoism. Taoism was formulated during the same period of philosophic speculation and political disorder as Confucianism; but it was a religion for the individual, not for society. The Tao is 'the way' of natural harmony; and if an individual could place himself on the way, in tune with nature, he was assured of happiness, long life, whatever he most wanted. Sometimes this search for natural harmony could be for evil ends, achieved by magic. Taoist priests assured their early imperial converts that their spells could offer them unlimited power (who could successfully oppose him if the emperor had the forces of nature on his side), or immortality. Chinese mythology abounds in Taoist sages mixing the elixir of life. Yet equally Taoism could lead to a religion of great kindness to men and animals who were fellow-travellers on the way. Or Taoism could be the religion of hermits who must be undistracted by the world in their search. However, in most educated men, Taoist principles of natural harmony merged imperceptibly into Confucian balances of propriety.

Buddhism, the only alien religion to become popular in China, established itself in another, later period of civil disturbance, 'the

Three Kingdoms', between the Han and the T'ang dynasties in the third century A.D. It was brought over the Himalayas from India; and one group of the Sutras was translated by six or seven men. There was a Hindu who knew no Chinese, but did know the scripture, a Parthian who could speak Hindi and Chinese, and four or five scholarly Chinese who spoke only their own language.

Buddhism and Taoism both became important religions for artists, writers, and artisans. Only educated men, or occasionally women, so the Chinese thought, could understand poetry or paintings. Philosophical historical, and religious education was needed to understand the allusions of poetry and painting and fill out the shorthand notes of the artist into his finished vision. Education was even more necessary for anyone wanting to write or paint themselves with the admired conciseness and restraint. In a painting of bamboos, or a literary mention of them, the educated saw wise gentleness swaying with the wind of change but not breaking. In the imagery of tossing willows sensitive artists described beautiful and changeable women.

In painting it was particularly important to know the Taoist mysteries and to be in tune with the natural scene. One should, said the Sung pundits, be able to chose a path, take a walk through a painting, and lose oneself. During the Sung dynasty particularly the great painters claimed that they needed the Taoist vision of natural harmony before they could work, a miraculous revelation of the path and picture they must paint. Taoist magic and spells were used in studios to induce this miracle. Even retired officials of the period who had been orthodox Confucians during their working life, were converted to Taoism when they turned to the arts in their old age.

However, in the centuries after the Sung dynasty the education needed fully to understand or to paint a picture became formalized. Inspiration and magic were partly replaced by pattern books of trees, mountains and lakes painted by the old masters. Court painters chose and carefully copied those appropriate to the emotions they desired to convey, and assembled them in their pictures according to the rules laid down in the book. Other painters, determined to show themselves amateur, made deliberate mistakes of technique.

A picture which was too perfect became the mark of the insincere artisan rather than the genuinely inspired scholar artists.

Buddhism's contribution to the Chinese artistic tradition was more popular, less acknowledged by Confucian scholars. When the first Buddhist monk from India, according to legend, arrived at the oasis of Tun-huang, on the western border of China, he had a vision in which he was told to dig a cave and establish a monastery. Later, as the monastery became one of the richest in China, the caves were painted in a curious mixture of Indian and Chinese tradition. Chinese-dressed T'ang courtiers standing around the T'ang emperor were edged by Indian demons. The Buddha on his lotus, as in thousands of Indian paintings, has around him Chinese dragons, Chinese-robed maids and a dark-skinned Indian groom.

The decoration of the caves continued for a thousand years from the Wei period of the fifth century A.D. to the later Sung. Most of the work was done by journeymen monks who travelled from the caves to other Buddhist temples painting and carving for their keep. The ideas they took with them from their contacts with India influenced painters, potters, and sculptors throughout China.

It was the duty of the Buddhist religious artists to show the Buddhas and scenes from their lives so that they were understood by the ordinary people; and the new skills spread from the models, carvings, and paintings of the gods to artistic work concerned with ordinary and court life, animals, and country scenes. At the end of the T'ang period the southern painters were producing the delicately detailed, botanically and zoologically accurate, paintings of insects and flowers which has since been one of the most enduring schools of traditional painting.

Buddhist priests played a large part in most funerals; and the transmigration of souls was the most comforting doctrine of life after death that the Chinese had. A Taoist hermit was a valued ornament to the country estate of a retired official with literary leanings. But both religions' most ardent followers were among the poor, and their influence grew in times of natural troubles. In the third century B.C., after a drought in Shantung, the Taoist crowds drifted in disorder over the province, singing and dancing to the Mother Queen of the West. (There were similar scenes during the Black Death in east Europe. However, on that occasion the starving dancers invoked the Virgin Mary as Queen of Heaven.)

By the eighteenth century it was rare for Buddhism or Taoism to play a major part in the religious sense of an educated man. Taoism had become above all the religion of bandits, and of semi-criminal secret societies. The members were bound to each other by magic oaths, and protected, so they believed, by Taoist spells. Both Buddhism and Taoism were associated with sexual licence in their monasteries and nunneries, and petty extortion from the poor.

However, in spite of the scandals of the past, for the last centuries of the empire the two religions were a tolerated and tolerating part of Chinese village life. Their gods shared the villagers' devotion with the ancestors authorized by the Confucian classics, and the yet older gods and ghosts of the particular neighbourhood. Buddhist, Taoist, and Confucian temples existed happily side by side; and people took a little of each doctrine to formulate their individual philosophies, so that they were able to regulate the ordinary details of their daily lives.

Most people, particularly the educated, used the balanced system of Confucian ethics. Confucius had laid down five personal relation-ships on which, he said, the welfare of the state depended. They were: subject to ruler, parent to child, husband to wife, older brother to younger brother, and friend to friend. Four of the relationships concerned Chinese private not public life, and three of them defined precisely the duties and obligations within the family.

In practice the most important relationship to a Chinese came to be that of parent and child, particularly father and son. A married woman (and it was a parent's duty to ensure the marriage of his daughter), lived with her husband's family. But for a son nothing could be too much to show his reverence for his parents.

A man who lost a leg or an arm in an accident might, in the Confucian examples, properly kill himself, because he had injured the body his parents gave him. It was a son's duty to sacrifice his life not only for his parents' safety, but also for their comfort or whims. His duty to them took precedence over any public duty. If the father of a good official should commit a crime, the son must take his old father on his back and they must both flee the state together.[7]

Ideally the Confucians envisaged a large joint family. Recent research has exploded the myth that this large family living under one roof was common.[8] (The average size of a twentieth-century, pre-communist, Chinese household was five, and so it probably had been in past centuries.) But the large joint families that did exist were important as a goal to which many Chinese aspired.[9]

These large families could consist of as many as 100 people living in connected courtyards surrounded by high walls. Most of the courtyards had several rooms built round them, including a living-room furnished with heavily carved tables, chairs, and chests. The rooms, if the courtyard was a pleasant one, opened on to an enclosed garden. The Chinese do not have the British passion for lawns; but where possible they plant small trees, often pines or bamboos, and they dig pools and divert streams to bring water into their garden. A 'full moon' bridge, high-arched, so that it and its reflection in the water make a perfect circle, is an admired garden ornament; so are curiously shaped rocks, and large pots of the flowers of the season.

The largest room in the joint family's house would be the hall in which hung the names of the ancestors and, if possible, their portraits. On feast days it would be the duty of all the family to watch the grandfather light incense on the central altar, and offer food and wine. Then, in order of family seniority, everyone present would bow to the ancestors and then to the older living members of the family.

The best and sunniest courtyard, where the grandparents lived, was generally close to the ancestral hall. Remaining courtyards housed married sons or male cousins, each with their own wife, children, and servants. Except on feast days each small family lived very much its own life, cooking and working separately. Each wife took her turn at attending her parents-in-law. The children played together, and shared a tutor. They were taught to call their cousins 'brother' or 'sister', and to honour their grandparents, uncles and aunts.

The least comfortable place in the family belonged to the youngest wife. Traditionally she had been married without seeing her husband, and she was under the strictest obligations to her parents-in-law. Her husband would have to divorce her if his parents complained seriously about her manners to them or her conduct. (It is perhaps not surprising that J. Lossing Buck discussing the population figures for Chinese villages in the 1930s, notes comparatively few women in their twenties and thirties. This was due, he concludes to the dangers of child-bearing and the number of suicides.)[10] But, if she survived, a grandmother became a matriarch, generally more concerned than her husband in the day-to-day ordering of the household, and honoured, rather than obedient to her sons and grandsons.

Very few of these large households lasted more than one or two generations. Even in rich families the death of the grandparents generally released each son to a separate house. But, like even the poorest of ordinary Chinese families, these households stayed part of a larger clan organization. These clans were for the majority of Chinese the bottom and most important layer of Chinese government. In the southern villages, particularly, one or two clans included all the villagers. The clan head was the senior man of the senior branch of the family; and there was also a clan council to govern the village. The clan cared for a joint ancestral hall, and kept genealogical books. It often provided for the education of able boys with poor parents. It ordered the farming of land, maintained local irrigation canals and paths, and collected taxes. All minor disputes between its members were settled by the clan elders.

Outside the clans the law was purposefully harsh. It was meant to punish only the most terrible crimes, to impress the people with the majesty of the state, and to discourage frivolous litigation. Plaintiff and defendant knelt throughout the case between a line of armed constables. Witnesses, whose evidence the magistrate doubted, were beaten on the spot. Chinese law refused to condemn a criminal except on his own confession. Torture was therefore used to extract these confessions. 'Severe' executions could be both cruel and prolonged.

Too many law cases were, moreover, a condemnation of the magistrate in charge of the district. Theoretically he governed by force of his own good example, rather than through his legal powers. He was exhorted to take a father's benevolent interest in his people, admonish rather than punish minor wrong doing, and reward the virtuous. It was a much prized mark of honour for an official tablet to be placed outside the door of a house where a large family lived in noted amity.

The good official, concerned with the order and happiness of his district, worked with the clans. He apportioned taxes and responsibilities among them; but he interfered as little as possible with their internal affairs and with individual quarrels. Reliance on the clans was necessary because there were anyway not enough officials for detailed administration. A population of about 100 million during the great dynasties was administered by 20,000 or fewer officials. (The Indian Civil Service under British rule had the same very low proportion of administrative officials to the total population. They were also encouraged to take a benevolent interest in the people they governed, but not to interfere in minor matters.)

The country was divided into provinces which were sub divided into prefectures, sub prefectures and counties. To avoid corruption officials were not allowed to work in their native provinces; and in principle they were moved into new districts every three years. The better the official the more often he was moved.

At the centre the emperor's ministers were there to advise him, and to be responsible for the different departments. There were dossiers on the whole civil service, reporting on their health, the good order in their districts, their characters, and their morals – particularly on their filial piety. An official could be executed for peculiarly shocking acts, like patricide, in his district even though he had had nothing to do with the crime. His example, it was argued, must have been bad.

Traditionally officials (foreigners called them 'Mandarins') were recruited through examinations of increasing difficulty in the Confucian classics. Each candidate was given two or three sentences from a classic to comment on, and a subject for an essay taken from

33

classical times. By the eighteenth century acceptable comment had become stereotyped. Candidates were expected to produce 'eight-legged' essays with the approved divisions, links, and summary of subject matter. In order to pass the examination candidates had not only to know most of the classics by heart so as to recognize quotations, but also to be so soaked in classical analogy and ethics that the proper Confucian sentiments came naturally to them when they were thinking fast and under stress.

The idea of a civil service recruited on merit through examinations dates back at least to the Han dynasty. Almost as ancient are complaints that the examination was too remote from the actual needs of government. Under the Sungs, in the twelfth century, the Prime Minister, Wang An-shih, tried to include in the syllabus questions on astronomy, law, philosophy and government, which candidates could not answer simply by classical quotations. But his reforms were not permanent. Nor were similar attempts at reform at the beginning of the Ming and Ch'ing dynasties.

China had no hereditary nobility on the scale of Europe's. During the interregnums, and in periods of imperial weakness, powerful families would increase their landholdings, their power over the tenants and the smaller people of the neighbourhood, and their central influence. But it was part of the policy of each new strong founder of a dynasty to break this sort of power. New nobles might be created from the new emperor's own supporters, but their ascendency was often limited to themselves or to the next few generations. The Ch'ing nobility, typically, operated on a descending scale, each generation declining one rung in privileges and rank. The same process happened automatically to those whose power was based on ordinary wealth or landholding. China, in striking contrast to Europe, had no custom of primo-geniture; or even of particular priority to the immediate family. A man's destitute brothers, cousins, and nephews might customarily claim part of his land equally with his sons.

Even in times of imperial decline, when a neighbourhood had both rich men and nobles, the local officials were more respected and, if any imperial power at all remained, more powerful.[11] A saying current during the decline of the Ming dynasty was 'The poor should never antagonize the rich and the rich should never antagonize the officials.'[12] Officials were even legally privileged, they were liable to different sorts of punishment, generally less severe, and they were exempt from forced labour. (This was the particular hardship that an energetic emperor inflicted on ordinary peasants.)

Wealthy landlords naturally had social advantages over their poor neighbours. They could hire substitutes for forced labour or army conscription. If the central government was too weak to exercise proper control, they could bribe, not so much the district magistrate himself, as his Yamen clerks. These small officials who were natives of the districts, unlike the magistrate, knew local conditions and were subject to local pressures. Their corruption was the constant complaint of their superiors. (Again compare British India: with the foreign, if uncorrupt, magistrate seldom aware of all the intricacies of the law suits he tried; an easy and frequent dupe for his corrupt local clerk.)

Under the Ch'ing the rich themselves became small local officials, and leaders of the '100 family' groupings with some legal power. They could also buy minor official standing; but only in the last and worst days of the empire did most of these bought offices carry any real government power with them.

In better times a family spent its money on buying education for its children. Those sons who could profit by it passed the official examinations and entered the bureaucracy. The stupid brother, incapable of passing the examination, was left to look after the family estates. If he could, he ran them from the neighbouring town, only going out into the country when he needed to collect his rents. Except in parts of Szechuan there was no Chinese tradition of resident squirearchy, interested in their tenants' lives, and withheld by ethical and neighbourly considerations from pressing them too hard. Nor was it part of Confucian ethics to be particularly sparing of tenants. A stupid brother or a land agent's first duty was to extract enough from the tenants, at whatever cost to them, to support the old and the official members of the family.

35

The prolonged schooling and the private tutors the rich could afford for their sons gave them an advantage in the examinations, but never an overwhelming one. Under the early Sung 46·1 per cent of officials were classed as coming from 'humble' families[13] (although how 'humble' and poor they actually were is not clear). The majority of officials at all periods came from comparatively prosperous families where their fathers, grandfathers, or uncles had also been officials.[14] The very highest officials were even allowed to enter a son into the bureaucracy without his passing the proper examinations. But the clan system and the encouragement of free or cheap schools meant that there was an opening for very poor boys. 'The blacksmith Chu-jun', 'the shoe-repairer scholar', were the nicknames of good Ming officials. Once in the system the poor boys would be given at least equal opportunity of advancement with the rich man's son. If the empire was at a peak of strength and order, possibly they were given even more opportunities. The poor boy who makes good is a hero very much in the Chinese tradition. Mere wealth and idleness were not considered to produce good characters (a belief in contrast to the common English assumption that gentle birth and rearing produce some merit even in the most stupid). A hard-working peasant's family, on the other hand, was, the Chinese thought, an admirable nursery for incorruptible virtue. Moreover most emperors considered it greatly in their own interest to encourage the scholar from the poor home. The rich and noble had other sources of power, the poor scholar depended entirely on the government.

Servants, who were absolutely dependent on him – poor officials without the ordinary connexions of the scholar gentry class, eunuchs, even men who had failed to pass the official examinations – were needed by a strong Chinese emperor. The emperors were isolated. In theory their power was absolute. The classics laid down that a supreme ruler was a necessity for good government. A concept, like that of medieval Europe, of the king as only the first among his equals would have been as shocking to Confucian Chinese as later concepts of kings restrained by Parliament or the popular will. Moreover a weak emperor endangered the position of the officials and exposed their estates to the raids of bandits and rebellions of the peasants.

Yet to the orthodox Confucians the strong emperors were dubious figures. In theory the emperor was a Confucian, yet it was not uncommon for a ruler restoring order to kill or exile most of his family. It was also in the imperial interest to reduce the inflated power of the gentry by tax and land reforms. Most of the emperors could, and did, quote Confucian and Mencian precedents for what they were doing, but their officials were still doubtful. The emperor was acting with un-Confucian forcefulness, and it was the estates of the officials themselves which often suffered.

The established channel for official criticism and reproof of the emperors was the Board of Censors. This was made up of distin-guished and elderly officials, many of them men whose courage stands out in the contemporary accounts. The emperors were likely to reward unwelcome advice with flogging, exile, or an unpleasant death. Less courageous junior officials could show a polite disagree-ment with imperial policies by resigning on one of the numerous grounds of bereavement or pressing family duties sanctioned by the Confucian code. Or an official could commit suicide after sending a letter of reproaches. (This had the additional advantage that his ghost would haunt the erring emperor.) But the official's own reputation and his family would be compromised, if he made no protest, tacit or open, about mistaken policies. He also endangered the peace of the country and the continuation of the dynasty.

Misrule could upset the balance of heaven and earth, and cause the emperor to lose his Mandate from Heaven: his right to rule. This mandate was conditional – very unlike the seventeenth-century European Divine Right of Kings to rule badly and still retain their thrones. While the emperor held it he was, whatever the practical tensions between him and his bureaucracy, the Son of Heaven. Rebellion was blasphemy. But once his mandate had been lost, whether by misrule or natural calamity, rebellion was justified and sure to succeed. (As in Europe, of course, the test of whether the emperor had lost his mandate was whether the rebellion succeeded.) Individually a servant of the fallen emperor might with honour remain faithful to him and to his family personally. (Many of the Ming officials refused to serve the first Ch'ing emperor.) But the duty of the scholar class as a whole was to secure the throne as an institution and re-establish earthly order. This meant that even the sons of an official, who had resigned when a dynasty fell, could with propriety and family approval serve the new emperor.

As Son of Heaven the emperor had a son's duties to sacrifice to his god-ancestors. If he neglected his religious duties, just as surely as if he neglected his civil duties, the balance would be upset, heaven's wrath would fall upon the country, and he would lose his mandate. For these religious duties the Ming emperors built the blue-tiled Temple of Heaven in Peking. At the winter solstice the emperor sacrificed a perfect young bull there to safeguard the farmer's year. In this, as in his other religious duties, he claimed ancestry from the Hsias, the imperial god-farmers. Like them theoretically, he grew his own grain for the imperial rites from a sacred field of god. It was ploughed ceremonially by the emperor himself and his ministers at dawn in winter. (They were dressed in traditional silk robes and high white court boots.) Each season he went to the appropriate city gate to welcome the new change in the farm year: the north gate for winter, the east for spring, the south for summer, and the west for autumn. In theory, during the spring, the empress gathered her own mulberry leaves from the palace sacred grove for her own silkworms. She wound the silk from them, spun it, and wove it. Then she embroidered the sacrificial robes herself, as the legendary Empress Lei-tzu had, and as a good farm-wife should. (In practice this time-consuming part of the ritual was delegated by busy empresses, like the nineteenth-century Empress Dowager, Tzu Hsi, to the junior concubines.)

From Chou times onwards there are records in Chinese literature of these rites, and of the way the emperors lived. There were great imperial palaces with walls enclosing gardens, lakes and hunting forests. Chinese building, however, is mainly of wood and mud brick. When a dynasty fell the old emperor's palace was generally sacked and burnt, often with the rest of his capital city. There was no traditional capital in China. The later Ming, and the Manchus (the Ch'ing) used Peking because it was close to their homelands and the centre of their power. But other dynasties had their capitals at Loyang, Sian, Hangchow, Kaifeng and Nanking.

Sian still has the remains of a small imperial palace. But the great Ming-built, Ch'ing-restored, palace at Peking is what both travellers and Chinese now think of as the heart of China. Traditionally, administrative buildings were within the palace or close to it. Under the Ch'ings, the Imperial palace, 'the Forbidden City', was surrounded by the Manchu city of Peking. Outside this city's walls was yet another city for possibly rebellious Chinese.

The Peking palace itself, behind walls of ochre red, is of paved courtyards, contained by marble steps and terraces. Each terrace leads into an open hall with pillars lacquered red, gold, green, and blue. The roofs are of shining yellow tiles, whose upcurves end in carvings of the dragons, unicorns, and phoenixes who guard the buildings. Until the most recent office blocks were put up, the palace was the highest building in Peking. Nobody could overlook the emperor. Even now its huge walls and gates still dwarf the people who walk through them. The lines and colours are sharpened and heightened by the clear, dry air during most of Peking's year.

The emperors furnished this most beautiful of palaces according to their very varied tastes. The halls were the living quarters of the imperial families as well as offices and audience chambers. They were heated by charcoal braziers, and hung with carpets, tapestry, and the imperial choice of pictures and objects of art.

The present Chinese government has turned the old palaces into museums for the imperial collections. These vary from the symbolic, poetic Sung landscapes, and the delicately detailed Ming court and hunting scenes, to the great bulk of knick-knacks amassed by Tzu Hsi in the nineteenth century. This formidable old lady professed a great admiration for her contemporary, Queen Victoria, and shared many of her artistic tastes. Tzu Hsi's clocks, statuettes, vases, and mechanical toys from home and abroad are now the much admired centrepieces in several of the Forbidden City museums, and in the Summer Palace, which she herself built just outside Peking.

There she was well served by her landscape gardeners who sited her halls, and the pillared walks linking them between hills and the lake, with twisting paths, bamboos, and flowering bushes round them. It was the last built and most romantically gardened of all the surviving historic buildings.

1 The tomb of Huang Ti (the Yellow Emperor), who ruled China in about 2000 B.C., has today been restored and re-dedicated to 'the father of the Han People'. This conjectural drawing of the emperor dates from the Chou dynasty (second–first centuries B.C.).

2 The Great Wall of China built during the Chou dynasty by Chi'n Shih-huang-ti is now considered a 'proud achievement of the working classes'. The primary reason for its construction was to prevent barbarians from entering Chinese territory.

氏轅軒帝黃

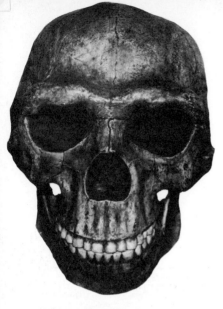

3 A reconstruction of the skull of Peking Man, who lived half a million years ago, represents the earliest known human-type in China.

4 This Neolithic Kansu pot discovered in China is about 7,000 years old and reflects the skilled craftsmanship of the Neolithic villagers.

5 The Shang dynasty produced many beautiful bronze objects including this ritual axe or jüeh which dates from the twelfth or eleventh centuries B.C.

6 This bronze bull's-head inlaid with gold and silver belongs to the Chou dynasty (c. 1027–256 B.C.).

7 Under the communist régime China's tradition and culture are respected by the young and old. Places of historical interest such as the dragon pavilions in Peihai Park, Peking are well maintained and much visited.

8 A modern young student copying a T'ang mural (sixth–ninth centuries A.D.).

9 Confucius (550–478 B.C.) formulated a philosophy which had a profound influence on the attitudes and beliefs of China's people. This nineteenth-century drawing shows Confucius with a disciple.

10 (*Below left*) By the time of the
Han dynasty (206 B.C.–A.D. 220)
Confucianism was the established
Chinese philosophy. A tomb paint‑
ing – 'Guests arriving at a funeral
feast' – from Liao‑Yang, Manchuria,
dates from this period.

11 Within a Chinese Confucian
society a gentleman's propriety, his
control and balance, was achieved
primarily through education. This
early photograph shows a scholar at
home studying for his examinations.

12 To be successful at examinations
was essential for social advance.
These private examination cells are
relics of a system which lasted for
many hundred years.

13 The South is a region of impressive scenery such as this landscape on the Lichiang River, Kwangsi Province.

14 The topography and climate of the different regions of China vary greatly. Cultivation on this land, in the West outside Chungking, follows natural terraces.

15 A principally Buddhist shrine shows an amalgam of symbols from other Chinese religious traditions including Taoism and Confucianism.

16 The local theatre has long been part of the tradition of Chinese village life.

17 Traditional observances such as the dragon-boat festival are still respected.

18 These Tibetan peasants are voting for their People's Deputies. Tibet has been part of the Chinese People's Republic since 1956.

19 Two languages, Chinese and Uighur, are used in the autonomous region of Sinkiang.

20 Livestock-breeding is a principal occupation among the inhabitants of Sinkiang. This is in the Ili River valley.

4   Rotting Tradition

'HEAVEN IS HIGH, and the emperor is far away', says one of the
most often quoted Chinese proverbs. For over 3,000 years the
dynasties came and went. Their collapse brought great misery to
the countryside. After the fall of the Ming dynasty in 1644, over a
million people were killed in the province of Szechuan alone. The
killing and chaos were worse still when there was a long interregnum
between the dynasties. Provincial barons struggled for overlordship
while most of them were unable to suppress banditry and the violence
of their soldiers within their own domains. It was a well founded
Chinese tradition, however, that such periods of disorder did not
last, any more than did periods of good order.

Even the foreign dynasties did not mark drastic changes of
direction in Chinese history. 'China is a sea that salts all the rivers
that flow into it', says one proverb.[15] The wife of the Mongol
emperor, Kublai Khan, wept, according to the tradition, as she
looked at the luxurious, imperial palaces of newly conquered
Hangchow. 'It came to me just now,' she said, 'that the empire of the
Mongols will end in this manner.' There were only small changes
even in ordinary life. The Mongols introduced trousers, wide-
brimmed hats, horse-riding and the blue and white pottery glazes
first developed in Asia Minor. Under the Manchus Chinese men
were made to wear their hair in long queues. There was always
some Chinese feeling against barbarian rule; yet, when a well-
established foreign dynasty was threatened by popular revolt, the
loyalty of most Chinese officials stayed with the Chinese-speaking,
Chinese-educated, only theoretically foreign, emperor and his court.

Much would be forgiven any government that did not interfere with the people. There are several versions of one of the oldest of the peasant songs:

> *I plough my ground and eat,*
> *I dig my well and drink;*
> *for King or Emperor what use have I?*

It was the government's duty, however, to maintain order that left the farmers free to drink from their own wells and eat the crops from the land they had ploughed. It was often better maintained order than in contemporary Europe. There were no dark ages of the length and destructiveness of those that followed the fall of the Roman Empire in Europe. While travel in the West was still dangerous and difficult the Chinese had good roads on which valuables could safely be moved, an excellent canal system, fast posts and well-maintained inns. Apart from bandits in times of trouble there was little crime or violence in imperial China. Laws were observed, and taxes collected, and remitted to the capital.

During the dynasties in which the civil service worked smoothly, notably the Han, the T'ang, the Sung, and the Ming, the arts flourished. Under the Sung, in their beautiful doomed capital of Hangchow, all of Chinese culture from poetry to cooking reached a new height. Confucian philosophy was debated, synthesized with parts of Taoism and Buddhism, and set in a form that was not to be broken until the end of the empire. The Sung built gardens, high houses, and temples round the lakes of Hangchow. The government was efficient, the court splendid. The Sung, however, despised war and military thinking. The emperors ignored the advice of their generals, provoked the northern barbarians, and made no sacrifices of their comforts or their city's magnificence to avert the Mongol menace which hung ever more threateningly over them.

Yet Sung art was in no way decadent. Since Shang times the Chinese have seen jade as a half magic stone: the symbol of purity and unbending virtue. Under the Sung the jade carvers were skilled enough to make realistic jokes: a miniature jade camel biting its own tail, an equally small tiger growling like a playful St Bernard's puppy. But, as in the other arts, technical skill had not under the Sungs become an end in itself. (Ming and Ch'ing artisans used jade, as they used lacquer and ivory, to show scenes of meticulous detail cut in deep relief. A bow string, the tie of a woman's dress, the separate corn stalks in a sheaf, were all separately carved out into a picture, often of greater interest in its parts than in its general shape and pattern.)

The Sung potters were as restrained as the jade carvers. The new glazes they used included celadon, a pure white, and a black glaze from Honan with brown markings. The potters used raised ornament on some of their work; but again the most ornate shapes, the dishes and bowls of several colours, the pictures on the bowls appearing as more important than basic form, were to be Ming and Ch'ing developments.

Lacquer work and embroidery were the two arts in which later technical skill showed to particular advantage. The carved lacquer of the Ch'ing is at its most impressive on a large scale, as it was used for the great imperial throne of Ch'ien Lung. Its red lacquer is inlaid with green and yellow, the imperial dragons writhe about the seated emperor, and a small elephant supports his back.

The Ch'ing textile workers used their skills both for woven and embroidered pictures; and for the robes of the emperor, his family, his servants, and his court. Only the emperor himself could wear the imperial yellow dragons on his long top coat (worn, according to Manchu custom, over high white boots), his nobles had a right to small dragonheaded roundlets on their clothes, his generals' robes were studded with brass dragon's heads. The women's clothes, like the men's in shape but not in colours or subjects of the ornament, were woven or embroidered with butterflies, flowers, or portraits of leisurely people.

By the time of the last Ch'ing emperors and the Empress Dowager, Tzu Hsi, nineteenthcentury China still appeared on the surface much as it had always been; peaceful, orderly, and traditional. Outside the few big coastal towns the country looked as it had for millennia. Every yard of arable land was handtilled; 'manicured', a visitor to China later commented. Villages centred every 20 miles or so on a small walled town. This was the market centre, the home of most of the local gentry and officials. It held the state granary for the grain offered as taxes. The town's narrow streets were lined with open-fronted craftsmen's shops where the goods were made by time-honoured methods. (A taut bowstring still powered the jade carver's drill.) Most of what the local people wanted was produced locally; but rare or foreign goods could often be copied or repaired. Some markets even had a stall which specialized in replacing the bristles of toothbrushes. Within their walls most towns had public baths, at least one good restaurant, and a number of teahouses. These served bowls of light amber-coloured Chinese tea, melon seeds and gossip. Many Chinese gentlemen, who were too educated to live on their own estates, but were not state-employed, spent a large part of their days in them.

Yet below this smooth surface of tradition nineteenth-century China was boiling with poverty and bitterly wounded pride. There were six major rebellions in the middle of the nineteenth century. The most serious, the Taiping ('the Heavenly Kingdom of Great Peace'), lasted 14 years from 1850 to 1864. For some of the time the imperial government lost control of South and Central China to the rebel administration. The Taipings only failed to topple the dynasty because the Chinese officials remained loyal to the Manchu emperor.

The Taipings killed thousands in every county and town that offered any opposition to them, and their suppression was equally bloodthirsty. The Viceroy Tseng executed all rebels in surrendering armies who spoke the dialect of Kwangsi where the Taipings had originated. Both sides massacred, and burnt villages and crops, for revenge and in order to hinder the movement of the opposing armies. In the northwest millions more Chinese lost their lives in the Moslem rebellions there. Barely a tenth of the population survived in some counties. Walled cities were left empty and ruined, and rivers polluted by corpses.

Partly because the rebellions and their suppression killed so many people the Chinese peasant's life was a little easier for a few decades in the later nineteenth century. The government encouraged peasant families to move into the devastated counties, and the growing pressure on the limited land of China slackened temporarily.

As early as 1740 the great Emperor Ch'ien Lung wrote: 'the population is constantly increasing while the land does not become any more extensive'. In the late fourteenth century there were about 65 million Chinese, under Ch'ien Lung about 200 million, and in the middle of the nineteenth century 450 million.

The government, in the classic Chinese phrase, 'lived off the backs of the peasant', and during the nineteenth century it became an increasingly expensive government. The tentative experiments at modernization, the foreign wars, and the foreign indemnities, as well as the increasingly corrupt and extravagant court with its hierarchy of privileged eunuchs, had to be paid for out of farms growing smaller as each generation was more numerous. The farms had also to pay the expenses of a tax system which encouraged corruption. Tax collecting was let out to the local gentry who were allowed to squeeze as much as they could out of the peasants under them, remit what was forced out of them to the central treasury, and keep their profit.

Taxes were made more oppressive by the balance of trade against China at the beginning of the nineteenth century. Silver was used to pay for imports; and its value rose in proportion to the copper coins which most peasants used to pay their taxes. Later in the century the world price of silver dropped, and the whole Chinese currency depreciated in terms of European currency. Between 1864 and 1874 the value of the Chinese tael halved.

There was no margin for even minor natural disaster in this economy. Landless and indebted peasants were driven into banditry. By the end of the nineteenth century dykes and irrigation canals were not being properly repaired because the treasury was empty, and local officials weak. The results of droughts and floods were magnified. In North China between 1877 and 1879 nearly 15 million people died during a drought, and were buried in what are still known locally as 'ten thousand men' holes.

In Europe similar population increases in the eighteenth and nineteenth centuries and similar rural poverty and discontent were part of the cause of industrial as well as political revolutions. In Asia itself Japan, China's neighbour just across the sea, had taken her first startled look at Western power when the American warships appeared off her coast in 1853. In the next 50 years Japan changed from a society more hide-bound and more medieval than China to one of the powerful, industrialized new nations. Her first major international appearance in this new role was her over-whelming victory in the Sino-Japanese war of 1894-5, and the Chinese humiliation in the Treaty of Shimonoseki which ended it.

China had a better supply of the raw materials needed for in-dustrialization than Japan. Her people have, over the last ten years, proved able to learn industrial techniques faster than previously untrained Europeans. In the early- and mid-nineteenth century she had a government administration which could have encouraged and enforced change. Among the rich there were periods of prosperity and men with spare money for investment. Oddest of all – until about the seventeenth century she had been the most advanced technically, as well as politically and culturally, of all the nations in the world. Through conquests by the Steppe peoples and the Arabs Europe had probably learnt Chinese skills as different as the use of stirrups and variolation (the predecessor of vaccination), and the techniques of using cranks, piston bellows, and water wheels. The Chinese printed their books, steered by the compass, made elaborate clocks, and used gunpowder centuries before Europe. (The myth, sadly, is wrong. Gunpowder was used in guns as well as in fireworks.) Chinese science, however, had no Roger Bacon. It was a matter of practical, empirical discovery to solve particular problems. Because men of education were not interested in scientific philosophy there was no working out of the principles from which scientific advance is made. There was thus no upsurge of knowledge re-thought and curiosity about the new in Ming[16] or Ch'ing China to correspond with the European Renaissance. China fell behind in scientific theory particularly. The first Jesuit missionaries to China were allowed to preach and hold official court positions because they made themselves useful as astronomers and mathematicians. 'As for the Western Doctrine which exalts the Lord of Heaven', the

Emperor K'ang-hsi wrote, 'it is opposed to our traditional teaching. It is solely because its apostles have a thorough knowledge of mathematical sciences that they are employed by the state.' (In the end K'ang-hsi expelled the missionaries and banned Christianity.)

During the eighteenth and nineteenth centuries the technological gap between China and the West widened. At first the Chinese did not even take seriously the new gadgets carried by this white-faced and foul-smelling[17] race of barbarian pirates. When Lord Macartney, George III's ambassador, arrived at the court of Ch'ien Lung, the old emperor saw his gifts as suitable tribute from a subordinate, but well-meaning, princeling. He examined the ingenious mechanical toys, the planetarium, the sprung coach, and the telescope. But the embassy's request that ports other than Canton should be opened to foreign trade was firmly refused. So also were Macartney's other requests for the regular exchange of ambassadors between Britain and China and the entry of Christian missionaries.

Ch'ien Lung might have listened with more interest to Macartney if he had been a less successful man. He had just defeated the Mongols in what was to be the last of the frontier wars. China's ancient enemies no longer menaced her, even the problem of the land shortage was temporarily relieved by settlement on the northern borders. Danger had never come to China from across the sea, Ch'ien Lung saw no reason to think this embassy marked a new epoch in China's history. 'We possess all things', was part of Ch'ien Lung's answer to George III. 'We are not interested in strange and costly objects and we have no use for your country's products.' His ministers assured Ch'ien Lung that if the strange embassy gave trouble the Europeans could easily be disciplined by stopping the rhubarb trade. Without rhubarb, it was believed in China, the Europeans would perish of constipation within months.

Even without rhubarb, there was much the Europeans, parti-cularly the English, wanted from China. The fashion for Chinese silks, porcelain, and lacquerware had reached its height in the eighteenth century. Many of the Ch'ing potters worked entirely on orders for the new market, making dinner services ornamented with the crests of British, French, and Dutch families. Chinese bowls and vases were painted with copies of European prints: harvest scenes, Prince Charles Edward in highland dress, Venus and her attendant nymphs.[18]

As always, foreign taste was unsure of itself in a new sphere. Foreign buyers encouraged the over-ornamentation and the sentimentality of Ch'ing potters and considered the multiplication of dragons, birds, and flowers to be desirable and typical of Chinese ware.

As the fashion for Chinese art waned towards the end of the eighteenth century, a new necessity, tea, took the carrying capacity of all the ships that could make the China run. In Ch'ien Lung's day the ships were allowed to load only on their built-up mud flat outside Canton where they could buy their goods through specially accredited merchants. They were guarantees to the officials for the foreign merchant's behaviour; and chosen for their own high character, supposedly, so as to stand between the population and the corruption of barbarian manners.

Meanwhile the European economists issued solemn warnings about the trade in Chinese luxuries and tea. The ships to China went out almost empty. The Chinese were paid with silver. Bullion, the economists complained, as the Romans had done before them, was being drained West to East. But the Chinese insisted that they wanted none of the products of Europe.

A few decades later the foreign merchants discovered opium, a commodity for which they could make a growing market in China. It was a particularly profitable trade for the British, because opium was widely grown in their new Indian empire. Ships could carry cloth and other British-made goods to Calcutta, load opium there, sell the opium in Canton, and then buy tea, porcelain and silk for the home run.

The fashion for chinoiserie was, however, ebbing. Chinese porcelain and lacquerware did not mix well with the fashions of the French Empire, with their stress on classical design and simplicity. Nor were the heavy, embroidered, Chinese silks as useful for the high-waisted, sheer dresses of the early nineteenth-century lady of fashion as they had been for her full-skirted, eighteenth-century mother. Tea continued to be a necessity in the West. But the

Chinese growers were increasingly undersold by the new planters in India and Ceylon. The introduction of opium into China was to tip the balance of trade even further against China.

In China the new drug rapidly gained addicts; and the Ch'ing dynasty prohibited the import of opium into China. The foreign merchants at first ignored the prohibition, and bribed the officials to let their cargoes in. In 1839, however, the special Imperial envoy, Lin, threatened to cut off the food supplies of all foreigners if they did not surrender their opium. He then burnt 20,000 chests of the drug. A few months later English warships in Canton harbour fired on Chinese junks. Other ships captured the ports of South China, and naval parties landed and took Nanking.

Both sides were astounded by the ease of the foreign victories. The British made very large demands in return for peace: the cession of Hongkong island, the opening of five ports to foreign trade, the payment of a large indemnity, and foreign officials to be given the same respect as was accorded to Chinese of similar rank. It was to be a model for wars and treaties throughout the next 70 years.

One European power after another, joined in time by Japan, fought China on flimsy pretexts. Chinese towns were sacked, Chinese armies were defeated. Chinese apologies for the war were tendered, and large indemnities promised. More concessions were then extorted about where foreigners could live and what special protection they should be given. In 1858 the countries concerned in the Treaty of Tienstin imposed 'most favoured nation' clauses on China, so that any concession made to a foreign country auto/matically applied to them.

Comparatively little Chinese land was ceded outright. But it was the heyday of imperialism, and each major power collected its own sphere of influence in China where its traders and missionaries were pre/eminent. The old expression of Chinese superiority over the outer barbarians was now balanced by European righteousness. In the mid/nineteenth century British merchants of Tienstin memorial/ized Lord Elgin. Europe possesses a mission, they said, 'to develop the vast resources of China, and to extend among her people the elevating influence of a higher civilization.'[19]

It is part of the communist argument now that the foreigners were largely responsible for the Chinese failure to industrialize during the nineteenth century. One of the most damaging concessions the Chinese were forced to make was foreign control of their customs. Foreign manufactured goods sold more cheaply in the interior of the country than those that could be produced in China itself. The old handicrafts died. Foreign silk, cotton, bowls, spoons, pictures and lamps were all cheaper and more popular in their imported forms. Artisans without work were then thrown back on the resources of their overcrowded farm families. Peasant poverty was added to as the handicrafts died. The old source of winter income, money earned, by the women of the family, spinning and weaving cloth vanished because imported Lancashire cotton from Britain cost less. Then, without the old skills, the farm families were no longer self-sufficient, they borrowed for their shop-bought cloth and lights, and the villages grew still poorer.

Meanwhile, in the cities, Chinese industries could not compete against the cheap imported goods. Most countries protect new industries by high tariffs until they can stand against competition. The Chinese could not do this. By the 1890s, after the Treaty of Shimonoseki, they were not even allowed discretion to tax goods made in foreign factories built in China.

Imperialism, so the communists argue, also encouraged a geographically unbalanced development of China. Foreign trade came into the seaports, and foreign factories were set up there, particularly in Shanghai and Tienstin. But there was little Chinese transport, east to west, linking the interior to the coast. Instead much of it, like the Grand Canal, ran north to south. The industrial coast was isolated from the main part of the country, and easier for foreigners to control.

Yet without the foreigners the technical and educational advances China made in the nineteenth century would have been even smaller than they were. Some Western institutions were deliberately copied. In the reforms of 1864 after the suppression of the Taiping, the only major administrative change of the century was made when a Foreign Office, the Tsungli Yamen, was grafted on to the old central bureaucracy. At the same time the first of the Chinese government modern schools were ordered to teach Western sciences and mathematics as well as languages. Chinese arsenals, and a shipyard were started, and ironworks and better transport planned.

The very wars against the foreigners forced the Chinese to consider the reasons for the easy foreign victories, and what they needed to copy in self-defence. After the 1879 and 1880 crisis with the Russians over the frontier post of Ili, when Chinese negotiations were made almost impossible by the rudimentary transport on their side of the frontier,[20] the Chinese started the North China telegraph line. Less directly militarily useful institutions, like the first Chinese-owned Shanghai cotton mill and the Imperial Bank of China, were set up partly with government capital to lessen China's dependence on foreign goods and foreign loans.

In spite of these efforts at reform, however, China continued to lag behind the West and Japan. She continued to be defeated with humiliating ease by foreign expeditions. In the eyes of the rest of the world she gradually became a comic-opera country whose armies carried umbrellas instead of guns, and where nothing worked properly. Her new industries often failed or produced shoddy and expensive goods. There was no large scale industrialization or adoption of scientific ideas, and peasant poverty worsened as the century went on.

Part of the trouble was that the nineteenth-century leaders (like Ch'ien Lung) could not believe that Western techniques were more than clever tricks: not connected with real education or a different scientific mode of thinking. 'Chinese learning as the basis; Western learning for practical use', was the quoted tag of the century. The good official or the good teacher, it was thought, needed a thorough grounding in the Confucian classics to which he could then add the necessary items of scientific technique or business management. Even in war the qualification for army command was still passing the examinations in the Confucian classics. 'The conduct of war rests with men not materials.' But it did not help Chinese resistance to foreigners when commanders in charge of the guns had had no artillery training.

It was almost impossible for a man educated in the Confucian tradition to accept another system of thought. In the reform period after the Taiping attempts were made to 'revive the ancient virtues', and make the examination system and the education leading to it less stereotyped. There was more emphasis on a candidate's general moral character and his grasp of contemporary affairs. But he still had to consider contemporary affairs in the light of classical precedent and precept; and qualifying papers demanded detailed knowledge of the classics. The serious candidate anyway had no time during his education to devote to reading outside his syllabus. Moreover most teachers regarded innovations in government or thought as in themselves wrong and impious. The natural balance existed. The Golden Age had existed. It was man's duty to find this balance and to recreate the Golden Age of the past, not to try for something new.

Towards the end of the nineteenth century more of the classically educated were showing some interest in Western learning; and their interest was reinforced by graduates from government modern schools and missions schools which made no concessions to Confucian ideas. But even these new men while they urged reform on the government were not themselves principally interested in science or mathematics, far less engineering or business techniques. They studied Western philosophy with interest, and to a lesser extent literature, history, even painting. But they were, even as rebels, still tied to the literary, unscientific, tradition of classical China. It was still unthinkable for an intellectual to work with his hands, or make the amassing of a great fortune of money his first interest.

In the West it had been the growing middle class which had directly or indirectly brought about most of the educational and economic changes of their countries' industrialization. In Europe, particularly in Britain, this middle class was a powerful and very self-confident group. Ever since the seventeenth century English plays and, later, novels contained references to the rich merchants who wanted their daughters to marry into commercial wealth not the decadent aristocracy. Equally they wanted their sons educated for trade and industry not as politicians or landed gentry. In nineteenth-century China these were impossible sentiments. There was a middle class of artisans and merchants in all the cities. But it had little political or social power, the wealth of its members was disapproved of, and in a way they disapproved of themselves.

There was in China no channel, like the English parliament or even the city governments, by which merchants could govern or even offer advice to the government. Their advice anyway would have been considered impertinent and likely to be tainted by the evils of their calling. In the official Confucian hierarchy the merchant ranked lowest of all – below the scholar, the farmer and the artisan. 'Exalt agriculture, disparage commerce', said the classic Confucian tag on the treatment of merchants, and it was faithfully followed by good governments from the Han to the reformers of the mid-nineteenth century. Commercial taxes were heavy and complicated and the official clerks expected bribes and presents from local merchants.

The despised merchants were not even considered the men best able to manage new commercial enterprises. As these were established in the late nineteenth century the typical form was a business jointly owned and capitalized by the state and a private merchant. (A pattern partially repeated by the communists' state-private businesses.) 'Official supervision and merchant management' was the phrase used; and the local magistrate and his office were expected to watch the merchant and control the low practices expected from him. The customs and caution of bureaucratic government were extended to these businesses; salaries and employment within the firm had to be found not only for the merchant's family, but also for official families.

Nevertheless, commercial fortunes were made in nineteenth-century China; first by Chinese compradores working with the foreign merchants, then by men who founded the first Chinese trading firms and commercial enterprises in the late nineteenth century. But the money these men made went, not as in the West into further commercial investments, but into enterprises which were, from the Chinese point of view[21] more established and respectable:

buying land or pawnshops, founding libraries or poetry societies. The sons of these rich men were educated not for commerce, but for official careers, and so for greater social esteem and power than their fathers had had.

By the 1890s the Empress Dowager, Tzu Hsi, had presided over 30 years of national humiliation and the decay of internal good government. The attempt, after the suppression of the Taiping, to revive the Confucian state had foundered. A modern industrial-ized state had not taken its place. In the provinces power was passing from the officials into the hands of local strong men. The state was almost bankrupt. The empress decided to resign in favour of her well-meaning, but not very astute, nephew, the Emperor Kwang Su.

A group of young men became Kwang Su's advisers, and in the summer of 1898 they carried through the Reforms of the Hundred Days. The literary examinations for the bureaucracy were to be replaced by examination in Western knowledge. Western-type schools and universities were set up in every province. The army and judicial system were reformed on Western lines. Machinery was to be imported and Western books translated. What roused particular opposition was the decree that officials, whom the reformers decided were useless, were to be dismissed. It was too much, too fast. The senior ministers petitioned the empress. She descended on the palace, stormed at the emperor, and had him imprisoned on a small island on the Lake in the Summer Palace. The Reforms of the Hundred Days were rescinded, and six of the young reformers executed.

Meanwhile a more popular protest movement was rapidly spreading among the peasants of Shantung, where a famine was attributed to the magic of foreign missionaries. The Boxers[22] at first included leaders who condemned the Ch'ing misrule as much as they condemned the foreign exploitation of China. But the move-ment of guards for the foreign Legations sparked-off riots, and the particular targets of the Boxers became 'the Primary and Secondary Hairy Ones'; the missionaries and their Chinese converts.

These missionaries of all churches had, by now, rejected completely the tolerant aristocratic ideals of the early Jesuits. They entered the country to convert the heathen masses, not the *élite*. They made no concessions to despised Chinese customs, and had, most of them, as little respect for Chinese law. Their converts were forbidden to join in the ancestral rites, and so broke their Chinese family ties. Away from the treaty ports the general ignorance about foreigners increased the unpopularity of the Christian doctrines. The stories that convents cared for unwanted babies in order that the nuns might kill and eat them, and that Chinese eyes were taken by foreign hospitals so that they might be used in Christian magic, long ante-date the communists. Most of the educated did not believe these stories, but they knew that the demands of missionaries, or the killing of a missionary living illegally in the interior of the country, were often the pretexts for foreign wars. In these wars missionaries acted as spies for their fellow countrymen.

It was, then, easy for the Boxers to gather recruits and support. They moved into Peking, almost unopposed, and the foreigners were besieged in their Legations. The Boxers depended on magic drills to protect them against bullets; but these were not efficacious against the foreign armies marching to the relief of Peking. About 15,000 Chinese and 475 Europeans were killed during the Boxer troubles, and the largest indemnity in history was agreed on. The sum of £67½ million was to be paid in 39 annual instalments.

Meanwhile, as the Boxers' fortunes had risen, the policy of the empress's government had wavered from condemnation to tacit and then open support. When the Boxers were defeated the empress fled from Peking to the ancient capital of Sian. On her return, in a desperate attempt to placate the foreigners and restore the popularity of her dynasty, she enacted most of the Reforms of the Hundred Days. Men were sent abroad to study. Legal torture was forbidden. Some of the useless officials were dismissed. At court the empress allowed talk of Western subjects, and received Western ladies. She was herself, she said, particularly interested in their underclothes and corsets. She thought they must be excessively uncomfortable.

It was, however, too late. The south particularly was alive with plots, secret societies and scurrilously treasonable rhymes on every-thing from the empress's dubious morals to the need to restore pure Chinese government and expel the Manchu usurpers.

The most prominent of the rebels was by now Sun Yat-sen, a young man from the district where the Taiping had started. He had been educated in the Western tradition, partly by missionaries and partly abroad. Many of the Confucian reformers who had survived the Reforms of the Hundred Days at first despised him, because of his extremism, the failure of his early attempts at rebellion, and because of his lack of any Chinese classical education. But his ideas were increasingly popular among the Overseas Chinese. Their communities sheltered Sun, and provided him with money for new plots to overthrow the Ch'ing government. Several amateurish attempts were unsuccessful, and Sun barely escaped with his life. Then, almost accidentally in the autumn of 1911, another rebellion was precipitated by the discovery of plotters in one of the houses on a Russian concession. There were soldiers' mutinies, provincial revolts, and widespread killing of Manchus. A republic was proclaimed in Nanking, and Sun Yat-sen elected its first president.

Some months after Sun and his new ministers went to the tomb of Hung-wu, the first Ming emperor, and made an offering of food, candles, and incense to him. His ghost was solemnly assured that the soil of China had been won back from the Manchus, just as the first Ming won it back from the Mongols. Chinese history was still, officially, continuous.

21 The Manchu Ch'ing dynasty ruled China from 1644 to 1911. This seventeenth-century engraving of the Ch'ing Emperors' palace in Peking reflects the eminence of his imperial position.

22 The administration of the Manchu Empire was in the hands of civil servants or Mandarins. This is a local magistrate's court of the period.

23 (*Above*) The religious activities of the Jesuit Matteo Ricci and his missionary colleagues were tolerated by the Chinese emperors because of their knowledge of Western science and astronomy. They helped found this Peking Observatory.

24 (*Below left*) Father Ferdinand Verbiest, a colleague of Ricci, was one of many Jesuits who emphasized the relationship between science and Roman Catholicism.

25 Ch'ien Lung who was Emperor from 1700 to 1799. He rejected proposals for alliance and trade made by George III of England.

26 Tea was an important export for China in the eighteenth century and became increasingly popular in the West. A nineteenth-century engraving of a tea plantation.

A.Humblot del.   Baquoy Sculp.

27 (*Left*) The Mandarins who were the backbone of imperial administration lasted until the Revolution of 1911. The house of a Mandarin from a nineteenth-century coloured aquatint.

28 (*Below left*) The importance of imperial China as an Asian trading country is reflected in this eighteenth-century vignette.

29 The passion for Chinoiserie reached a peak in the eighteenth century. This plate inscribed with an English coat-of-arms was made for export only.

30 Lacquer work was an art in which the Ch'ing craftsmen excelled. A Ch'ing table top dating from the eighteenth century.

31 The enforcement of the Chinese prohibition on the import of opium precipitated the war of 1840 fought against Britain. This nineteenth-century engraving of the capture of Chumpei by the British dates from this period.

32 The war ended with the signing of a number of agreements which established the 'treaty ports'. Shanghai was one of these. A nineteenth-century anonymous oil painting.

33 The narrow streets of old Chinese towns were lined with craftsmen's shops.

34 Missionary zeal towards China reached a peak in Britain during the nineteenth century. This Protestant missionary was one of many who attempted to evangelize the heathen masses as distinct from the *élite* – the earlier aim of the Jesuits.

35 (*Above left*) Traditional methods of coal mining in about 1900; this crude winch was operated by man-power only.

36 (*Above*) Silk-spinning in the open air. The manufacture declined in the nineteenth century because Chinese silk was undercut by foreign silk.

37 (*Below left*) Between 1877 and 1879 nearly 15 million Chinese people died during a drought. Primitive irrigation systems like this man-run wheel were not adequate for the growing rural population in times of poor rainfall.

5 The Communists

SUN YAT-SEN'S GRAVE is a place of pilgrimage in today's communist China; and his widow, Sung Ching-ling, is one of the vice-presidents of the state. But how close to a communist Sun was himself is doubtful. Like many of his left-wing contemporaries in Europe, Sun admired the new communist state in Russia, was curious about its social experiments, and thought it had much to teach the world. He saw, however, the most pressing of Chinese problems as those of the land and the peasants, not of factories and workers; and communism, before Mao, had small place for agricultural societies.

Nevertheless, when Sun died in 1925 the Kuomintang was officially a coalition. The small Chinese Communist Party, born in the post-revolutionary turmoil, had Russian advisers who urged co-operation with the Kuomintang to bring about Chinese unity and independence. Bourgeois revolution in China, the Russian theorists argued, must necessarily precede communist power. However, Sun's successor, as leader of the Kuomintang, was Chiang Kai-shek. Chiang had been reared in orthodox Confucianism (although after his marriage to Sun's sister-in-law, Sung Mai-ling, he became a Methodist). He was determined to establish a strong, unified, and non-communist China. North of Canton, the centre of the Kuomintang's power, the country was divided among warlords. Chiang led a successful army north. In Shanghai in 1927 he turned on the communists. Those who did not escape into the deep country of central China, were killed, sometimes after torture. Communist and left-wing provisional governments were suppressed; and Chiang and the new right-wing Kuomintang were both powerful and very popular.

The young communist agitators who had followed Chiang's first army, or struck out on their own, had alienated popular feeling. They had mocked the old, and shouted 'Down with Cannibal Confucianism'. Landlords had been killed without the formality of trials, or finding out whether they were good or bad of their kind. Peasants had watched these killings without taking part in them. Even the subsequent redistribution of land had been ill-organized and ineffectual. In this young rabble there was little to appeal to the moderate or scholarly Chinese.

Chiang on the other hand had unified the country. His government was more orderly and more in accordance with tradition than that of the warlords; and there were promises of yet better government to come. In return for his break with the communists he had the support of Chinese and foreign businessmen, foreign loans, and the hope of extracting further solid concessions from the foreign powers.

Less than 25 years later only a handful of Chinese followed Chiang to Taiwan (Formosa). Most of his army had deserted him without even fighting. As well as the Chinese peasants, the great majority of the rich, the scholars, and even the civil servants who had once worked for him, preferred to welcome the advancing communists. Chiang, his relations, and the rump of his party were bitterly, and personally unpopular. The last days of his government were compared to the worst periods of the classic interregnums. The Kuomintang was condemned for failing to fulfil its promises of reform, failing to understand or help the needs of the country, and failing to fight the Japanese.

The promises the Kuomintang made in its early days were based on the three principles of government Sun Yat-sen had written into the testament he left his party. They were Nationalism, that is national unity and independence; Political Democracy, not immediately but in three stages; and the People's Livelihood, or economic reform. Specifically Sun had called for land reforms and state investment in industrialization.

Economic reform, at the time of Sun's death, was urgent. The increase in peasant debts and the pressure of population on land which had been partly responsible for the troubles of the later empire and its fall, had grown worse under the warlords who had taken power over most of the country after 1911. Paper money had been issued recklessly and the peasants forced to accept it. Savings had lost their value, or been looted by bandits, or official and semi-official soldiers. Army pay was generally months in arrears, and in order to live the soldiers had to rob the countryside. Taxes, however, continued to be collected years in advance.

Even after the Kuomintang had established itself over the warlords as the lawful government of all China, the peasants enjoyed only some of the benefits of peace and order. There continued to be local bandits. Those Kuomintang officials and troops who did reach the villages, demanded bribes, conscripted boys, raped and murdered. 'You do not take good iron to make a nail, or a good man to make a soldier', said one of the traditional proverbs. It is often quoted in accounts of life in the Chinese country under the Kuomintang.

In the 1930s China had some of the worst floods and consequent famines of her recorded history. The landlords' holdings and rents increased as families sold their land in the effort to keep alive. Interest rates went up. R. H. Tawney noted that 40 to 80 per cent was common, 150 to 200 per cent not unknown. A moneylender who charged only 25 per cent was known as 'a blessing' to his village.[23] Where they could the peasants crowded into towns already plagued by the world wide unemployment of the time. They could not beg effectively because the professional Guild of Beggars was more skilled, and adept in discouraging competition. Instead they sold their younger children for household slaves or prostitutes. Then they sat on the edge of the pavement, keeping their clothes and feet politely out of the way of passers-by, until either the police moved them on, or they died of cold and hunger. The Shanghai municipality hired carts to go round the streets at dawn picking up the night's tally of dead from the gutters.

Yet, during the 1930s, the Kuomintang was not the government without all hope that it was to become. After the break with the communists and the economic troubles of the time, the Kuomintang had lost most of what working-class and peasant support it had ever had. But its members still included representatives of the numerically small, but growing, new middle class of the eastern towns: missionary and foreign-educated technicians, business and professional men. James Sung, Chiang's father-in-law, had been one of these new businessmen with an interest in such untraditional ideas as educating his daughters. Chiang's brother-in-law, T. V. Sung, was a powerful financier, no radical, but interested in a more powerful and modern China. Partly under his influence the Kuomintang set up reform commissions. Bright young men, Chinese and foreign, were employed as advisers and public relations officers, some welfare legislation modelled on Western prototypes passed, and even a few model factories opened.

It all resulted in very little. Too many people had to have too many cuts from each new scheme. Chiang is said personally to have been incorruptible. This was not true, however, of those close to him. It was too easy to bribe one's way out of inconvenient new welfare schemes, and government-sponsored investigations. It was not even as if Chiang himself had put reform at the top of his list of priorities. His main interest, whatever other schemes the Sungs persuaded him to agree to, remained his army, placating the rich men who paid for his army, and the suppression of his opponents in China, particularly the communists.[24]

Yet with all its difficulties, economic and personal, avoidable and unavoidable, the Kuomintang would have made a more respectable government without the external menace of Japan. After Japan had enthusiastically and successfully accepted Western techniques during the nineteenth century, she also wanted an empire, and an assured market for her new industries like the Western powers. She chose China as her colony.

In 1931 the Japanese army took over Manchuria. Japanese troops were moved, more or less with Kuomintang consent, into North China; and in 1937 Japan had a reason for open war there, when Chinese troops shot back on the Marco Polo bridge outside Peking.

Long before 1937, however, Chinese young people of any education were in no doubt as to who was their national enemy. There were incidents in the cities when students organized anti-Japanese boy-cotts, and attempted to burn the entire stocks of shopkeepers who displayed Japanese articles. In the clashes with the Kuomintang police some of the students were killed, and feeling against the Kuomintang policy of appeasement mounted.

Yet Chiang continued to say that it was necessary to achieve internal unity before attacking the Japanese. After the first fighting around Peking, the Japanese met only token resistance in their conquest of northeast China. Shanghai was bravely defended; but after its fall the Kuomintang was driven back, over the mountain ranges, into the far interior to make their wartime capital in Chungking.

There were Chinese who wondered whether the Kuomintang, like the old dynasties before them, had lost the Mandate of Heaven. But the men who still thought in these Confucian terms were outmoded. The early communists shouting 'Down with Confucius' had shocked the villagers of the early 1920s; but 15 years later the breach with the Confucian past, the ideas that had inspired China for over 2,000 years, had widened.

The beginning, in the late nineteenth century, had been the gradual whittling down of Confucianism before the new ideas, the success, and the self-confidence of the West. Confucianism, instead of being the one and only system of ethics and government, the universal truth for all civilized men everywhere, shrunk to being only the Chinese truth. Confucianism, its partisans asserted, was the Chinese contribution to the wisdom of the world; an equal partner with other great truths like Christianity or Islam. Chinese thinkers desperately searched the classics for proof that the scientific and cultural ideas of other continents were to be found in China too. Alternatively Confucianism was defended as the national essence of China. Without it the Chinese would be disorientated, a people without historical roots.

These were half-way positions; they were still further eroded by the rejection of Confucian education as the qualification for government administration. The young men, educated at modern schools, blamed the old ideas for the humiliation of their country;

but they did not know what to put in their place. In the intellectual ferment after 1911, educated Chinese considered most of the world's philosophies. Christianity failed to fill the vacuum because of its associations with Western imperialism. John Dewey and Bertrand Russell lectured to enormous and enthusiastic audiences during their visits to China; and there were many adherents of the new rule of rationalism and liberal humanism. Yet, as with Christianity, the political precepts associated with these beliefs suffered from association with the West. Moreover, the Chinese did not relish being other countries' pupils. They wanted a set of beliefs and practices they could make their own.

To this intellectual hunger Chiang's Kuomintang offered a warmed-up hash of muzzy Western ideas and the discredited past. The Confucian virtues, Chiang said, could save China. His official hero was Tseng Kuo-fan, the Viceroy who had suppressed the Taiping and attempted to restore the old order in mid-nineteenth century China. Ladies in silk dresses urged modesty, austerity, and restraint. But it was only possible to warm the Confucian flesh, not to make the whole skeleton walk again. Confucian education could not be revived. Kuomintang China needed technicians, not philosophers. Nor did the old examination system for the appointment of officials replace nepotism, bribery, and the degrees of Western-style universities. The intellectual promises of the Kuomintang in China were as empty as their promises of practical reform.

The communists had more satisfying fare to offer. Their intellectual origins in China were with the New Tide discussion groups of Peking University around 1919 and 1920. The professors who led these groups were attracted to Marxism partly because the orthodox West had rejected it as a workable political idea. Moreover, the only country which then proclaimed itself Marxist, the Soviet Union, was only partly European. The communist revolution had already led to more emphasis by the Russian leaders on their Asian role, and the brotherhood in this new society of Asians and Europeans. Just after the revolution, the Soviet Union, the only European country to have done so, had voluntarily renounced its concessions in China.

Communism, as it developed in China, grew recognizably less German and Russian, more Chinese, closer to Chinese problems, and phrased in Chinese idioms. The architect of this Chinese communism was Mao Tse-tung, the son of a moderately prosperous Hunanese peasant. As a boy Mao had insisted on going to a modern college in Changsha, the provincial capital, and at that period a seed-bed of young revolutionaries. Several of his fellow students were to become leaders of the Kuomintang or the Communist Party. Many of them planned to study abroad, but Mao was too poor. Instead he found himself work in the National University of Peking. (In 1949 when the triumphant communist armies entered Peking the University hung out a banner 'Welcome back to our Assistant Librarian'.) He joined a New Tide discussion group, and in 1921 he was one of the dozen delegates who founded the Chinese Communist Party.

Mao was well read. Chinese history and novels provided him with analogies he used constantly in later books and speeches. But with his shambling, untidy appearance, his loud laugh, and the voice and many of the tastes of a Hunanese peasant (he still likes the fiercely peppered food of his native province) he did not seem like an educated, influential man. The part he played in the foundation of the early party was less than that of the slicker, city-bred young men who were friends of the first Russian advisers.

After the Kuomintang killing of most of their leaders in 1927, the Central Committee of the party continued to try and bring about a revolution on orthodox lines through strikes and revolts in the cities. In 1928 Li Li-san, the then leader of the party, voiced the danger that Chinese communism might become 'contaminated' with 'peasant mentality'. But city revolts were bloodily suppressed, and their leaders took refuge, when they escaped, in the villages. Even there embattled but untrained peasants were easily defeated by regular soldiers. Mao Tse-tung organized the Autumn Harvest Rising in his own province of Hunan in 1927; and he only just escaped after its failure to the mountains of Chingkangshan in South China between Kiangsi and Hunan provinces. In these mountains, and in similar inaccessible strongholds throughout the country, communist troops were trained, and communist methods devised.

In his 1927 *Report of an Investigation into the Peasant Movement in Hunan*, Mao had already stressed the dominant part he thought peasants must play in the Chinese revolution. He wrote:

'The force of the peasantry is like that of raging winds and driving rain. It is rapidly increasing in violence. Every revolutionary comrade will be subject to their (the peasants) scrutiny and be accepted or rejected by them. Shall we stand in the vanguard and lead them, or stand behind them and oppose them?'

In Chingkangshan and the neighbouring soviets, Mao's position was strengthened, as the old city leaders of the party were killed, fled to Moscow (as Li Li-san did in 1931), or forced to take refuge with him and agree to his ideas. One of Mao's earliest recruits was the reformed warlord, and ex-opium addict, Chu Teh. He became the commanding general of the Red Army, and he and Mao remained unbreakably loyal to each other through the early leadership crises. To the surrounding peasants and foreigners the commander of Chingkangshan was known as Chumao: one man, an undefeatable new kind of political bandit.

It soon became clear that Chumao headed a formidable army. In striking contrast to the Kuomintang army Chu Teh and his officers wore the same uniform as their troops, ate the same rations, and did not ride when their men had to go on foot. From the beginning political officers were attached to each unit. It was their duty to see that the soldiers understood the army's part in the revolution, teach them to read so that they could follow Marxist pamphlets, and impress on them the importance of good relations with the surrounding villagers. The soldiers were forbidden to take a needle from a peasant's house without paying for it; and they were ordered to help with farm work anywhere they were billeted.

Political education was not confined to the army. The local peasants were encouraged to kill their landlords, and redistribute the land under communist guidance. There were mass literacy campaigns. Opium, prostitution, child marriage, and forced betrothals

80

were forbidden. In return the peasants provided recruits for the Red Army, supplied them, and when it was necessary hid, spied, and fought with the soldiers. Because of this peasant support Chu Teh and Mao worked out guerrilla tactics which enabled the soviets to survive four major offensives planned by Chiang Kai-shek's German military staff. 'The enemy advances: we retreat. The enemy halts: we harass. The enemy tires: we attack. The enemy retreats: we pursue.' Mao wrote about Red Army tactics.

However Mao's military tactics were over-ruled by other leaders in a Fifth Campaign. A Kuomintang army of 900,000 troops blockaded the soviet and moved inwards under heavy artillery and air cover. All villages that could supply the communists were burnt; and all peasants – men, women, and children – found in areas friendly to the communists were killed. (At least a million civilians are believed to have been killed or starved to death during this white offensive.)

In the autumn of 1934, in the face of their defeats, the communists decided to retreat. They broke out of central China, westwards, into country that was not heavily garrisoned. Then, during the Long March that followed, their goal became the only surviving large soviet in north Shensi. Their route lay along the borders of China, through country almost impassable, and inhabited by tribespeople who, before, had fought any Chinese army impartially because they saw all Chinese as aggressors.

In October 1934, the Long March began with 90,000 men and a handful of women. During the next year this army walked about 6,000 miles. (There were a few horses reserved for the most important leaders and the wounded – Chu Teh's peasant wife carried extra wounded on her back.) They took, temporarily, 62 cities that lay in their path, crossed 18 mountain chains and 24 large rivers. Hostile tribes, notably the Lolos, shot at Red soldiers but were converted to helpful allies by the promise of favoured treatment when the revolution was successful. On the whole the Red Army moved faster than the Kuomintang and so avoided pitched battles, but there was fighting, in north Kweichow and over some of the river crossings.

At the Tatu river, in the far west, the bridge had been destroyed by the Kuomintang army; but soldier volunteers swung themselves, hand over hand, across the chains which still hung above the river gorge. The pass over the Great Snowy Mountain farther to the north was 16,000 feet high, and the army had no warm clothes with them. Many of them were barefoot. On the marshland, on the Shensi border, men who strayed from the path were sucked under, and died before they could be dragged out. Others died there from exhaustion and fever. But the organization of the Red Army was not broken, even though only a tenth of the men who had set out, about 7,000 of them, and 30 women, arrived in Yenan, Shensi.[25]

The whole epic of the Long March became a source of pride, not only to communists, but to other Chinese looking for some national achievement, to place against the Japanese victories. For the communists in power after 1949 the Long March became a major inspiration for all arts. Mao himself wrote several poems about it.[26]

There are now exhibitions of Long March paintings; a museum map of the route with illuminated buttons to highlight the sites of heroic incidents; and children learn to read from simplified *Stories of the Long March*. A recent opera, *The East is Red*, included a ballet of soldiers miming in semi-traditional dance style the obstacles in the way of the Long March army.

Politically Mao's position was greatly strengthened by the Long March. Shensi was a more secure and a bigger base than the southern soviet had been. On the march north Mao, by political intrigue and out-arguing his rivals, established himself as supreme leader, not only of his own soviet and its army, but also of the delegations and reinforcements from other smaller soviets along the way.[27] After the march the survivors were united by particular loyalties to each other and to Mao. 'A Comrade of the Long March' has been one of the few reasons accepted for sentimental actions in communist China.

The avowed aim of the Long March had been to bring the Red armies into fighting proximity to the Japanese. The outspoken hostility to the Japanese (and of the Japanese to the communists),

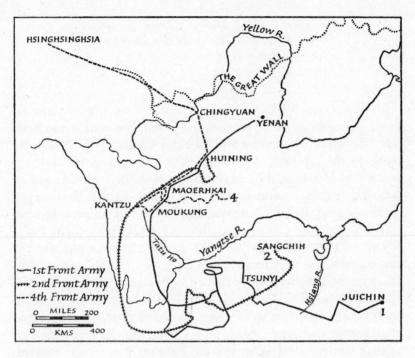

The route of the Long March

had become a major attraction of the movement for young Chinese. But the new Shensi soviet was soon surrounded by the Kuomintang; and Chiang ordered his generals to give top priority to wiping out the 'bandit remnants', not to fighting the Japanese. One of the armies he sent to the Shensi front was Manchurian soldiers under the command of the young Marshal, Chang Hsueh-liang. Chiang, however, was warned of the discontent in this army, sown by communist agents, and added to by patriotism and the stories of Japanese atrocities in their Manchurian homelands. He flew up to the Shensi front on a surprise visit of inspection, and, in what is still one of the most disputed incidents of the civil war, was taken prisoner in Sian by Marshal Chang in 1936. On the walls of the pavilion where he was held, someone wrote later:

A great thieving animal was caught here
but it was let off when we discovered
that it was no wolf,
but a jackal.[28]

In China now Chiang is represented as having been in a state of
terror during the Sian negotiations. His death, however, would have
been the signal for anarchy over much of China, and a swift conquest by the Japanese. The communists and Chang Hsueh-liang
knew this. Moreover, the communists knew of the United Fronts of
left-wing parties against fascism then being formed in Europe.
Stalin wanted the old Kuomintang-communist alliance revived
and believed that Chiang was the only leader who could unify
China. An agreement between the three leaders was published a
few months before the formal declaration of the Sino-Japanese war
in 1937 and there were to be further negotiations. (Chiang insisted
that the Manchurian Marshal Chang Hsueh-liang should go back
to Nanking with him to be court-martialled there. It was a secret
trial; but 12 years later Chiang took Chang Hsueh-liang with him
from a mainland prison to one on Taiwan. Chang was released
after 24 years in 1960. He had served a year for every day of Chiang's
imprisonment.)
    The Sian agreement had only a limited value. After less than a year
of war the swiftness of the Japanese victories ensured that the Kuomintang and communist front lines were cut off from each other
by a large area of Japanese-held territory. The communist and
Kuomintang both organized their own, separate, anti-Japanese,
resistance movement among the peasants. The communists had a
particularly effective system of underground tunnels in North
China, so that Japanese troops could be taken by surprise, and
villagers hidden from Japanese revenge. Towards the end of the war,
over most of North and Central China, the Japanese held only their
forts and the main towns, while the communist underground controlled the country.[29]
    As the war went on communist resistance officers complained that
Kuomintang agents preferred to betray them to the Japanese rather

than to help them. Both the Kuomintang and the communists accused the other side of intriguing against their armies, and no Kuomintang supplies were passed to the communists. Nor did the communists receive supplies from Russia. Stalin told visitors that he considered the Kuomintang the proper government of China.

The Chinese communist armies used wooden cannons they had made themselves, wound round with telephone wire stolen from Japanese country. The villagers in the resistance made their own mines filled with stones. The army wove its own clothes from the wool of Shensi sheep. What medical supplies there were were improvised; microscope slides from broken window panes, eye droppers from old rubber hoses, and a surgical instrument sterilizer from an old gasoline container.

There was the same sort of improvisation throughout the communist areas. In Yenan, the communist capital, everybody, including Mao himself and the rest of the leaders, lived in roughly furnished caves hollowed out of the loess cliffs of Shensi. There was a university in the caves with home-made and shared equipment, and books, schools, hospitals, administrative headquarters, and a clothing factory. (The stolen telephone wire again: this time used for looms.)

The foreign reporters invited to Yenan, and smuggled in despite Chiang's prohibitions, reported the improvisations, the atmosphere of equality and comradeship, the fervour with which the war against Japan was talked of and fought. There was, too, little but good to be reported about communist methods of government. Land had been re-distributed in Shensi, but without the violence and killing of the landlords that had gone on in the southern soviets. The new peasant owners generally lived better than the government officials. The army was disciplined and apparently popular, the leaders spoke gently of gradual plans for China, and of coming to terms again with the Kuomintang.

It was all a marked contrast to Chungking. Foreign supplies were brought into Kuomintang China at great cost in lives and money. For most of the war they had to be flown in from India over the Himalayas. These supplies were duly labelled 'medical' or 'ammunition', but when the boxes were accidentally opened too often they contained cosmetics or imported clothes for the wives of officials with most influence in the government. Meanwhile the hospitals were as short of supplies as those in the communist areas, and the ordinary soldiers worse armed and clothed. There was corruption everywhere, growing worse in the introverted atmosphere of wartime Chungking. The most moderate critics of the régime were imprisoned, or, if they were better known, assassinated by undetected criminals. The Kuomintang leaders were remote, arrogant, and lived in great comfort and grandeur.

Behind the mountains in Szechuan Chiang and his government were dependent on the taxes and food brought in by local landlords. These landlords were naturally implacably opposed to any reform of the system of landholding or lowering the rents; and the Kuomintang was now removed geographically from the possible reforms the more modern common sense of the seacoast businessmen had once suggested. Policy and promise for the future grew even more conservative, and more closely allied to the landlords' interest.

The contrast between the corrupt, ill-administered, and unhopeful Kuomintang, and the moderately-spoken, efficient, and egalitarian communists, was obvious to all Chinese who read the foreign reports, heard rumours, or were able to see for themselves. Young Chinese, particularly students, who were able to escape from Japanese-held towns increasingly went to Yenan not to Chungking. Other Chinese, who were not communists, and who as landlords, businessmen, or Western-oriented teachers, had interests that seemed to conflict with communism, nevertheless saw the communists as the new hope of their country.

For a few months after the end of the Japanese war in 1945 Chiang appeared to control the major part of the Chinese mainland with the communists shut up in an unimportant northern area. But it soon became obvious that, as with the Japanese, the Kuomintang controlled the towns, but the communists the country, at any rate in North China. Meanwhile, further Chinese sympathy was alienated from the Kuomintang by the rapidly spiralling inflation brought on by their simple economic policy of paying for rising war costs and the equally rising cost of corruption by printing more, and yet more, money. Housewives carried suitcases filled with the almost worthless paper dollars to pay for their day's marketing. Salary earners rushed out with their month's pay to convert it, preferably within the hour, into durables with fixed values, gold or American dollars.

Chiang himself apparently saw no need to make more than paper promises of reform and token changes in his government. He resigned as president, only to accede to the popular clamour he himself noticed for his own recall. His American advisers and associates were more and more outspokenly critical of him. They advised peace, conciliation, and immediate land reform; but their government continued to supply the Kuomintang with arms to use against the communists. After 18 months of uneasy peace Chiang started a new offensive and Yenan fell. It had, however, already been evacuated by the communist armies following Mao's old guerrilla policy of retreat in the face of head-on force. But it was the last time he was to use these guerrilla tactics.

In the communist counter-offensive of 1948 Manchuria collapsed in a few days and the Kuomintang armies there either surrendered, together with their new American equipment, or retreated south beyond Mukden to be reinforced by the best troops Chiang could send. They were defeated in the three weeks battle of Hsuchow, and in February 1949 Peking fell.

Chiang boasted that the communists could never cross the Yangtze, and in the spring of 1949 there was a short pause for further fruitless negotiations. On the night their ultimatum expired communist armies crossed the river without more than token resistance from the Kuomintang. In May they entered Shanghai. All over China Kuomintang armies surrendered without fighting. Canton fell. Chiang, his family, some of his army, the contents of the museums at Nanking, and a great deal of money went to Taiwan. The museum treasure, some of the most beautiful pictures and ceramics in the world, were lodged for a number of years in damp caves. The money went into American securities. The Formosans found themselves with a government of mainlanders of whom it was later said that they 'had learnt nothing and forgotten nothing'.

In Peking on 1 October, Mao read out the proclamation of the People's Republic of China from the Gate of Heavenly Peace: the entrance to the imperial palace of the Mings and the Manchus. 'Our nation will never be an insulted nation', Mao said. 'We have stood up.'

38 China suffered severely during the China War in the 1860s against Britain and France. The Taku forts were (wrongly) believed by the Chinese generals to be impregnable.

39 The Boxer Rebellion of the 1890s was primarily against foreigners, but the movement gained some of its strength from the general discontent. In 1900 the rebels besieged the foreign legations in Peking, leaving them in ruins.

40 (*Left*) Sun Yat-sen is acclaimed as a hero by both the Nationalists and the communists. He founded the Kuomintang and was the progenitor of the 1911 revolution. 41 (*Right*) His successor was Chiang Kai-shek who is still President of the Kuomintang in Taiwan.

42 The Second World War was for China the continuation of a war with Japan which had started in 1937. The city of Chungking after Japanese bombing.

43 Western influence and Japanese troops during the Second World War.

44 A haphazard civil war raged between the communists and the Kuomintang during the Sino-Japanese war. The communist centre was at Yenan. This capital with its simplicity, improvisation, and leaders who hollowed out cave dwellings of the Loess hills, captivated the imagination of many young Chinese and visiting Westerners.

45 This wall drawing was part of the anti-Japanese propaganda promulgated by the communists.

46 The civil war went on after the end of the Second World War. In 1948 these trenches were manned by Nationalists who had temporarily forced the communists to withdraw.

47 Some of the results of the civil war: homeless refugees and defeated Nationalist soldiers.

48 During the Sino-Japanese war the communists and Kuomintang had formed a United Front. The symbols of both parties hang either side of a village theatre demonstrating anti-Japanese tactics.

49 Volunteers of the People's Liberation Army receive their orders.

50 There was an outward expression of enthusiasm and contentment among the younger communist factory workers. This is at Wu-Chi-Cheng in North Shensi.

51 A Kuomintang school of the period.

52 A Chinese Soviet workers' club room in the 1930s dominated by rough portraits of Marx and Lenin.

53 Anti-Kuomintang feeling was expressed in communist propaganda posters.

54 The civil war lasted until 23 April 1949, when Nanking was liberated by the People's Liberation Army. Nanking waits to greet the victors.

55 (*Below right*) The last session of the Nationalist government in July 1949 before the People's government took over on 1 October.

56 Chiang Kai-shek, his superior officers and the rump of the Kuomintang fled to Taiwan. These are some of the officers waiting to leave.

57 In July 1949 General Chin-yi dominated by a portrait of Chu Teh, one of the leaders of the Red Army, inaugurates a celebration of liberation.

6   The New Men

IN THEIR TRIUMPHANT SWEEP SOUTH the communists marched through crowds whose cheers, flags, and appropriate slogans had been carefully organized for weeks beforehand. But the enthusiasm was partly genuine. Nothing could be worse than the past; and the discipline and efficiency of the Red Army and the new local governments made a most favourable first impression.

The Red Army contrived to pay for its stores. Its officers were not arrogant towards the civilian population, and stayed in full control of their men, even after the fighting. The first local officials were often these officers, or the political commissars attached to all army units. If they were civilians they were trained to be equally humble in their first approaches towards the civilian population. A Shanghai presbyterian minister told me, six years later, that his first co-opera-tion with the communists had been secured by a hiking expedition, organized for his Church Youth Group, and led by some of the new officials (cadres). What had particularly impressed him, he said, was that the cadres had washed the feet of the youngest members of the party every night.

The civilian officials had a uniform as functional and as un-splendid as the army's khaki. Their high-collared blue tunic was originally Sun Yat-sen's uniform for his followers; but most of the Kuomintang had dropped it years before or wore it in a well-cut woollen form. The uniforms of most of the young men from Yenan were patched and faded. They were meant to look poor, and like the poor, they wore padded tunics with cotton waste in winter not wool.

The new women cadres wore the same uniform as the men. Their hair was cut straight in severe bobs or swung in long pigtails down their backs. None of them wore make-up. They worked with the men, and lived in the same barracks. A few cadres married each other; and in theory, and very largely in practice, there was no sexual activity of any kind outside marriage. If two cadres of opposite sex walked back alone in the dark from a meeting, or were seen to be holding hands, they would be publicly criticized, and one of them would probably be posted away to another administrative centre. It was a matter for restrained boasting, particularly in front of Western visitors, when one of a married cadre couple could say that he or she had been separated from their spouse for several months or years. They worked in different towns, and they were glad to make this 'sacrifice for the revolution'. Besides, a conscientious official had little time for married life. Every hour of the day had its allotted activity; and periods for sleep were severely restricted. It was part of the ethos, encouraged by novels and newspaper articles of the period, that a cadre should cut into these hours yet further for his work or study. The communist myth was that it was a mark of the really good cadre to be able to do without sleep altogether for several nights on end.

Adultery, fornication, sloth, and drunkenness have continued to be among the least favoured vices of the communist society. Gluttony in recent years has been less frowned on. Officials say that Chinese cooking is part of their national inheritance, and so it is ideologically correct for good restaurants to continue; and for official banquets to be sumptuous with traditional Chinese cooking.

In the early days, however, the men and women cadres ate in communal dining halls which served food of varying qualities – the best and the most meat for the highest officials – but even for them less good and less varied meals than the town middle class were still able to afford. Junior officials swept and scrubbed for themselves and kept all their personal possessions in small unlocked cupboards. They were scrupulously clean: unhealthily so, many of the poorer Chinese thought. One of the least understood of the Red Army's propaganda lessons in Yenan had been that peasant mothers should wash their children, all over, every day.

It was extremely difficult to bribe these austere young people.

Even if they had wanted to be corrupt they had no private place to keep the bribes offered them, and no leisure to enjoy luxuries. Most of them were anyway well trained by the schools and universities of Yenan, and were high-minded to the point of priggishness. A Shanghai father told a foreigner that he and his family had prepared the most magnificent meal they could assemble for their son, returning with the Red Army from years of hardship in the north. They had made up his bed in his room, and asked his old friends to meet him. Only under orders from his superior officer would the young man agree to visit his family at all; and then he refused to eat the meal prepared for him, or sleep on his old bed. 'Rice and bare boards,' he said, 'are all I need now.'

The government these new men and women brought was to begin with, moderate. At first, in the conquest of Manchuria, unpopular Kuomintang officers, landlords, and factory owners had been publicly beaten or summarily executed. But this open, random violence was soon clamped down on when the communist leaders saw the damage it was doing to their image of national unity. The new government, Mao declared, was to be a 'People's Democratic Dictatorship'. There was to be 'democracy for the people, and dictatorship for the reactionaries'. The reactionaries were the landlords, the closest associates of the Kuomintang rulers, and 'bureaucratic capitalists'. (One definition of the bureaucratic capitalists later given to me was that they were Chiang's relations.) The petty bourgeoisie (that is the small shopkeepers), the national bourgeoisie (for instance factory owners), and the intellectuals (including those in professional occupations) were grouped with 'peasants' and 'workers' as part of the 'people' whose unity the new state should secure, and whose rights would be safeguarded. In the Chinese People's Consultative Conference which met in September 1949, the bourgeoisie were represented by members of the established political parties, including a dissident branch of the Kuomintang. But the leaders of the new society, it was said, were to be workers and peasants; and their official representative party in the Conference were the communists.

In practice this meant an amnesty for most ex-members of the

Kuomintang. Army units who had deserted during their retreat were incorporated into the Red Army, sometimes together with their officers. Members of the Kuomintang civil service were told to report to the local government centres, and then carry on with their old jobs. In the towns the first concern of the new government was to make life as normal as possible. Public services were got going again after the considerable damage done by the retreating Kuomintang. The local radio stations broadcast a continuous stream of reassurance and orders aimed at civil peace and security. Shops, banks and factories re-opened quickly. Businessmen continued to run their old businesses, except that the central government was now producing long lists of regulations for them about working conditions, welfare, and minimum wages. The most resented of the new regulations restricted an employer's right to dismiss workers without union agreement and heavy compensation. But the restrictions did prevent unemployment and destitution in the slump that, in Shanghai particularly, followed the government's first months in office.

This slump, and the government's control of monetary inflation, made life in many ways easier for townspeople. A new, more stable, currency replaced the old. The sale of gold and dollars except through a bank became illegal. Taxes were high and efficiently collected; and great pressure was put on everyone with surplus money not to spend it, but to buy victory bonds. Some of the first well-publicized executions in the towns were of black marketeers; but with exit permits rigidly controlled, there was no longer the same point in sending money out of China, or holding it in a form, like gold, which was easily transportable. In Shanghai, however, where groups of foreigners stayed on, there were to be small black-market transactions in currency for several years to come.

What struck visitors to China under the new government was how quickly the communist officials had put their own impress on what were supposed to be the ineradicable customs of China. For ten years to come visitors from China were to tell stories about what they had seen, which the 'old China hands', the businessmen who had lived in Shanghai and the treaty ports, contradicted flatly as 'impossible'. It was 'impossible' that begging, theft, and prostitution should have vanished from the Chinese city streets. But prostitutes, beggars, and petty thieves were rounded up into special camps on the city outskirts, officially sympathized with as victims of society, and trained in new occupations. The most distinguished guests of the new state found, sometimes to their indignation, that there were no prostitutes at all available. Unlocked trunks were left untouched on crowded railway stations. Hotel servants ran after departing guests with old socks, discarded into wastepaper baskets, and zealously retrieved. Tips for this, or any other service, were proudly refused.

It was only possible for the government to stamp out crime because they had also stamped out the old secret societies. By now these societies, common to every town in China, had become associations of gangsters tied together with a certain amount of Taoist magic and rites which were supposed to secure their members against the police. The old China hands, however, were sure that, where the British and French had been unsuccessful in stamping out secret societies in their far eastern empires, the communists could not have succeeded.

They were equally incredulous about the physical cleaning up of the Chinese cities. After the first months the contrast between the dirt and litter of the Hongkong streets, and the somewhat drab cleanliness of Shanghai and Peking, was remarked on by most travellers. In the new China the cadres had formed associations of local women whose job it was to be responsible for sweeping the pavement outside their homes and keeping the neighbourhood generally tidy. One of the first officially sponsored campaigns was to get rid of flies, rats, mice, and sparrows. (But the campaign had to be hurriedly backtracked when crops were eaten by field pests whose numbers were no longer kept down by the sparrows.)

The drabness many visitors complained about in the cities was added to by the general adoption of the cadre's blue uniform by both men and women. Blue cloth, for a time, was the only sort available in the shops. Even for those whose old clothes were still good, the revolutionary blue was useful protective colouring when silk or patterned cloth might otherwise have been picked out as evidence of counter-revolutionary sympathies. Women also adopted the female cadre's hair styles. Not having permanent waves or lipsticks was officially said to leave them more time to devote to Marxist study and revolutionary work. Only the wives of the capitalists, the factory owners of the big towns, were encouraged to go on curling their hair. Their husbands were expected to wear Western dress with a collar and tie when talking to officials or foreign visitors. These were slightly derogatory marks of the capitalists' class status.

By 1950, however, the towns had not changed radically. Without inflation and with the new social legislation, there was no longer the starvation and destitution among the very poor that there had been. But the people who had managed the towns continued, by and large, to manage them, and stayed better-off than the people who were and had been their workers. There had been few arrests or executions for political reasons as yet, and below the surface the changes were not dramatic.

In the country it was different. There were fewer surface changes. Country peoples' clothes did not change, and there was little crime or prostitution in the villages to get rid of. But from the very beginning of the revolution landlords were outside the national partnership. The first job of the new cadres as they moved into each of the villages was to decide who were the landlords, and to group everyone else in the village into the officially defined classes.

Landlords, even if their holdings had been no larger than a suburban garden, were those who had let their land without working it themselves. Rich peasants worked their land with the help of hired labour. Middle peasants had smaller holdings which they worked almost entirely themselves with, perhaps, occasional help. Poor peasants had the smallest holdings, probably rented; and they might supplement their income from their own land by working for rich peasants or landlords. At the bottom of the old pyramid, or at the top of the new communist social structure, were the hired labourers.

It mattered immensely into which class an individual fell. Landlords not only lost their own land and their personal possessions to the poor peasants (although they might, if they were not judged guilty of some other offence, keep the same amount of land as the poorest villager for their own use); but they also lost their civil rights, and their children were discriminated against in schools and in selection for the universities. Rich peasants kept their land, but were officially disapproved of, and likely to be suspected of crime in any period of government repression. Poor peasants and hired labourers, like the skilled workers in the cities, were the official beneficiaries of the revolution. (Eight years later, at the time of the Hundred Flowers, there were bitter complaints that the cadres had misjudged individuals' class status.)

The poor peasants did benefit from the first land reform. At the end of it their holdings were slightly larger, and many of them had an extra quilt or cooking pot from a landlord's house. But there was an overall land shortage in most of China. The landlords' holdings, however they were divided, were not enough to raise the poor peasants to anything like the level of the rich peasants, or to what, in Europe, would be regarded as a reasonable standard of living.

The cadres' teams moving into the villages were instructed to live in the houses of the poorest peasants, if possible; identify themselves with their sufferings; and rouse them against the landlords. Land reform was not to be carried through until the majority of the whole village demanded it, and the peasants were encouraged to deal with the details of re-distributing the landlords' property themselves. Among the advantages of this, from the point of view of the communist leaders, was that more of the Chinese population played a positive part in the revolution, and therefore would be in danger if the Kuomintang returned.

After his property had been re-distributed, the cadre encouraged the peasants to bring the landlord to trial before a 'People's Court'. This was a crowd of local people who denounced the landlord for real, or partly real, or wholly imaginary, crimes, and shouted for his death or imprisonment. No evidence was heard except the yelled denunciations; and the landlord was pressed with blows and curses to confess to his crimes. 'Dig, dig the bitter roots. Vomit the bitter water,' was the slogan the cadres shouted as the people remembered old grievances. Some executions took place immediately. The trials were broadcast and heard in Hongkong where they made an extremely bad impression. But ever since the time of the trials there have been disputes about just how many landlords were involved, how many tens of thousands were shot, and how many of these were men whose oppression of their tenants had been truly criminal. The communists have since acknowledged that 'mistakes' (in other words wrongful executions) were made at this period; but ex-landlords, concealed landlords, and fugitive landlords, are still today the popular villains of Chinese communist mythology.

7 The Unified State

THE VISITOR FROM HONGKONG hears his first Chinese slogans come over the loudspeakers of the border station, and then over the loudspeaker piped to every compartment of his train to Canton and Peking. The station staff, says the loudspeaker, 'under the inspired leadership of Chairman Mao and the Communist Party of China' have raised their production level by 3·8 points. Their five-year plan will now be fulfilled in three years, ten months and five days. In the visitor's hotel the room stewards do not at first answer their bell because they are just finishing their meeting on raising their production levels. They have each of them unanimously agreed to clean 3·4 extra rooms a day. They were, the steward tells a visitor, 'inspired by the glorious example of Chairman Mao and the Communist Party of China'. He is speaking half-forgotten English without any witness present to report what he says to his questioner.

Elsewhere university professors, pedicab drivers, businessmen, a few of them again speaking without a witness or an interpreter present, have also raised their production levels, thanks to the same, identically inspired, leadership. The few visitors to China who have friends they knew before the revolution, find that they too quote the raised production levels, the same slogans expressed in exactly the same pattern of words.

Suddenly the pattern changes. There is a new slogan. The station staff, the room steward, the professor, are all 'walking on two feet', or 'consulting the experts', or 'exercising Red economy and thrift to safeguard the national heritage'. By traditional methods, and consulting their oldest staff member, an elderly porter of impeccable peasant ancestry, the station staff reveal that they are making an excellent substitute for axle grease out of swamp mud. The room stewards, by the same methods, have found out how to make reed brooms that clean the rooms with a minimum of expense. The university professor has been told about a neglected, effective, and cheap drug from the pharmacopoeia of traditional Chinese medicine. There is the same quotation of exact, decimal-pointed, statistics, and the same leadership thanked for the new inspiration they have given. In the past raised productivity was introduced into every conversation, however unlikely the opening seemed. Now inquiries about a parent's health, the working of a machine, the popularity of a picture, all produce the same references, ingenuously worked round to the new dominant themes of economy and traditional knowledge.

This uniformity, this absence of any individual point of view, far less complaint, is overpowering to most Westerners. It has been achieved by a national pattern of life in which there is nothing that is outside politics. Correct political attitudes and changes in political attitudes are taught in classes at schools and colleges, and at meetings for adults. In the autumn of 1964 *Small Friends*, a Shanghai publication for very young children published a song it thought apt for the times and suitable for the age of its readers. It went:

> *There is an evil sprite,*
> *The name is Johnson.*
> *His mouth is all sweetness*
> *But he has a wolf's heart.*
> *He bombs Vietnamese cities*
> *and kills the people.*
> *Chinese and Vietnamese are all one family.*
> *We will certainly not agree to this.*
> *I wear a red scarf*
> *and join the demonstrations with Daddy.*
> *With small throat but large voice I shout*
> *'US pirates get out, get out, get out.'*

Older children have classes occupying up to a quarter of their schooltime on the political theories and philosophy of Marx, Lenin, Stalin, and Mao; and on the history and achievements of the

Russian and Chinese communist parties. Bad reports of a student's political attitudes can prevent him getting the sort of work his qualifications merit; and make him or her into an object of permanent suspicion and surveillance from local political officials.

Adults attend meetings for political 'study'. These meetings may take several hours every evening, or be held only once or twice a month. It depends on the status of the individual; (the more intel-lectual his work the greater the number of meetings); and whether the period is one of political change. At their simplest these meetings consist of readings from newspapers and official handouts explaining policy. Everyone at the meeting is expected to listen carefully enough to report back the substance of the article, and to learn by heart the important slogans contained in it. The slogans are echoed in loud-speaker announcements, piped out not only at railway stations but in workshops, restaurants, or the stairway and lavatories of a block of flats. Banners with the same slogans are put up everywhere. Films and novels, as well as newspaper articles, are hurriedly produced to repeat the slogans and illustrate their practical application.

A play I saw in Shanghai was about a scientist horrified at the misuse of some of his work to support American germ warfare. He finally departed in a blaze of music and strong light to fight with the Chinese volunteers in Korea. But much of the interest of the play lay in its illustration of how political vice or virtue appeared in every aspect of life. The wicked College Dean showed his wickedness, not only in his actual treason, but in his long old-fashioned Chinese gown, reactionary in contrast to the heroic cadres' blue uniform. He had long, and again reactionary, finger-nails. His furniture was reactionary, Western style with lace antimacassars; so was his food, Western again; his wife's dresses; his abrupt manners to his servants; his own traditionally devious conversation. The play drew its biggest laugh from the audience when the hero, misled by the wicked dean, said, puzzled, 'surely science is more important than politics?'

The communist political lesson is not only that nothing is more important than politics, but also that political considerations must decide every action of life . . . and dominate every second of one's time. 'He who believes that spare time is private time lacks the correct attitude towards the revolutionary cause', said the Peking *People's Daily* 14 years after the establishment of the revolution. 'One must spend one's leisure hours strengthening one's ideology and improving one's work.'

It is wrong to scold a child in any but political terms, to lay out a garden for any but political reasons, or to enjoy a poem, picture, or film for qualities unconnected with the political lessons it teaches. This is a totalism reminiscent not only of Confucius and the laws of proper behaviour that must underlie every action of the gentleman; but also of the character training of a good girls' boarding school in England. In the boarding school, as in communist China, every action has its iceberg of political or ethical content. The girl who eats extra sweets, like the Chinese who buys black-market sugar, has committed not only a minor breach of the regulations, but also an ethical or political sin of magnitude. It could not have been committed if the Chinese, or the girl, had been in tune with the régime, or the Spirit of the School, and had fully accepted its teaching. Therefore the crime is as potentially revolutionary as throwing a bomb at the Mayor of Shanghai, or knocking down the headmistress. It must be analysed, preferably in public to rub home the lesson, in order that the criminal may seriously and sincerely repent, and others take warning from his or her example.

Public and private scolding is at least as effective in the Chinese state, as it is in an expensive English school, in producing the desired uniformity of action and thought. In the streets of Chinese towns it is the traffic policeman's duty, not to summons offenders, but to lecture them before a growing crowd until they acknowledge their faults. Young red-scarved Pioneers on buses reprove their elders for spitting. Cadres at public meetings scold those who have failed to read the right books or voice the right thoughts.

People who refuse to go to meetings (or refuse publicly to acknowledge their minor political faults) are likely first of all to be visited by delegations from their colleagues. They will be asked why they will not go, what is wrong with the meetings, what suggestions they have to improve them. The delegations will be patient, humble, and persistent. Listening to them and answering them will take more time than actually going to meetings.

A girl who had recently left college in Shanghai told me that when one of her fellow students failed to attend political meetings, and allowed his work to lapse generally, a group of his former friends were told by the cadre to go and see him. 'We stayed from supper until dawn with him once,' she said. 'When he told us to go away, we went, of course, but we always came back.' The young man finally agreed to attend meetings in future, and made a public confession of the faults in his general attitude which had led to his recalcitrance. 'His father had been a mill owner,' the girl told me. 'He had been unable to escape from his bourgeois background.'

Most Chinese from time to time have to make public criticisms of their past lives, and public confessions of their faults. For anyone with a pre-revolutionary middle-class background the confession is expected to include a denunciation of parents, teachers, and family habits, and an analysis of mistaken views at work, in their marriage, and towards their children. The audience of this self-criticism is expected to help the man or woman making it by pointing out faults he has omitted or the full seriousness of which he has failed to understand. Anyone who fails to emphasize a friend's faults to him publicly is himself liable to public criticism as a hidden enemy of his so-called friend and of state security. The traditional importance the Chinese have put on 'face', on a man's public image, make these public criticisms particularly painful; and the public denunciation of parents and teachers are outrageous by Chinese traditional standards. To the authorities the pain and outrage are a necessary part of the criticism. They mark the subject's decisive break with the past. He can no longer be the same man with the same standards as he was before. His only future is with the new, communist, standards.

Many of these public self-criticisms are made during one of the periodic campaigns against groups of people the authorities considered were, at that time, particularly vulnerable to non-communist thought, incorrect communist thought, or even counter-revolutionary thought. These campaigns have sometimes been called purges by the outside world. But the word 'purge' with its under-tones of physical brutality and mass murder is misleading. Since the government established itself in the early fifties there have been very few political (or criminal) executions in China.

In later campaigns those successfully denounced have often not even been imprisoned. The aim of the campaigns, the communists say, is not only to safeguard society but also to correct wrong thinking and to reform a section of the people – the mistaken individuals exposed by the campaign. Even for those imprisoned the state's first aim is reform. Death sentences since the early fifties, have generally been commuted for two years, to be carried out then only if the individual has not reformed. Reform in prison is shown, as it is out of it, by hard work in the prison factory, attention in political study groups, thorough self-criticism, and a denunciation of past associates and crimes. Few of the commuted death sentences, visitors to Peking and Shanghai prisons are told, need to be carried out.

Torture, in the ways in which it was used in Nazi prisons, in Stalinist Russia, and in Kuomintang China, is rare, if it is used at all. But the communists, and most of the prisoners they have released into the Western world, do not count 'physical methods of reform' as torture. Prisoners may be chained to encourage them to recant. One of the American women who were imprisoned in China had been kept in chains for most of two years. 'But they were light chains', she said on her release, 'and it was for my own good.' Other prisoners are kept short of sleep during their interrogations, and they may be beaten by their cell-mates whose duty it is to 'help' them recant and make a full confession.[30]

In the later campaigns, particularly the campaign against the intellectual critics of the Communist Party after the Hundred Flowers period, sentences to Labour Reform, or Labour Surveil-lance, were more common than prison sentences. There are Labour Reform camps attached to some state farms, and to some public works like the big irrigation schemes or new buildings in the far west. The people serving sentences work under guard. As in prisons the length of sentence and the severity of working conditions varies according to how genuine a prisoner's repentance is believed to be.

Some Western newspaper stories, particularly in America, say that forced, unpaid labour has built most of the new public works in China. The existence of Labour Reform camps on an enormous scale, involving millions of prisoners, is implied. No traveller in China has found evidence supporting these stories. Public work is to be seen all over the new state, but prisoners under guard working on it are a rarity. Probably these stories of the vast slave camps are founded on the difference between the Chinese and the Western interpretation of 'voluntary work'.

Peasants and townspeople are expected to work on public build/ings or irrigation schemes in their neighbourhood. The work is voluntary. Sometimes it is not paid, or badly paid; and very often the people who do it are expected to carry on with their ordinary farm work or city jobs in the time they have left over. People could refuse to do the extra work in theory. In practice a refusal to volunteer would involve whoever made it in the same sort of unpleasant, time/consuming and shaming process a refusal to attend a meeting involves.

Apart from Labour Reform those judged guilty in the 1958 and 1959 campaigns of a lesser degree of 'rightist thought' were often sentenced to work under supervision, sometimes in country com/munes, and sometimes in a menial capacity in their old town work/places. During these campaigns large groups from town offices, who were volunteers, not those individually denounced, were in any case sent to the villages to work on the land. They were expected to live as the peasants lived, eat the same food, and not try to clean or tidy up their rooms beyond the peasant standard.

The theoretical reasons for this enforced, but often temporary, migration are that townspeople are thus given an opportunity to learn from the doctrinally purer peasants and 'reform their work styles' by ennobling physical labour.

Sentences to Labour Reform and Labour Surveillance follow meetings of great bitterness: 'struggle meetings', where the accused are shouted at, sometimes hit, and denounced by their closest friends and relations. The confessions following these meetings in 1958 and

1959 were published in detail in the Chinese press. They were couched in abject and humiliating terms, particularly considering the former status and age of the men and women confessing. In the session of the National People's Congress, at the height of the campaign, the former ministers and their followers, who had criticized the Communist Party, confessed. A Western witness saw one of them, an elderly ex-minister weeping, and noticed that Prime Minister Chou En-lai, on the Praesidium pointedly ignored him, and went on talking and laughing with his neighbours.

Recent reports from China suggest that the campaign against the critics who had availed themselves of the Hundred Flowers was concluded in 1960. Afterwards the pendulum of permitted opinion swung a full-length back and forth. There was first a campaign against 'leftist' over-enthusiastic Communist Party members, and then, recently, a new campaign against rightists. This time they are called 'Revisionists', after Krushchev, and they are those who advocate softer policies and the weakening of class war.

Earlier campaigns and propaganda drives were aimed at groups whose thinking and organization fell outside communism. The family itself, the most potent group in pre-communist China, was never the subject of a direct campaign after 1949. Instead Chinese communist youth newspapers urged on young people their duty to support their old parents. *King Lear* was quoted in all seriousness by one young people's magazine as an example of decadent Western family life of the sort that would not be found in China.

Yet the family was weakened. After 1911 it had lost most of its legal powers, and now its members were encouraged to take disputes short of the law to the new welfare organizations rather than to the arbitration of senior relations. Moreover the prestige of the old in the family was inevitably lessened by the rapidity of technical as well as political change. Experience of the China of 40 years ago was a disadvantage, not an advantage, in the new state. What was wanted now was youth, and quickness to learn, politically and technically.

Much of the intensity of old-fashioned Chinese family life had depended on the utter absorption of women by their families. This was attacked by one of the first laws of the new government. Women were given equal legal rights with men, including rights to refuse a distasteful arranged marriage and rights to divorce. For a time the courts were crowded with women victims of the old system. Meanwhile women cadres urged other women to free themselves from 'feudal shackles' to their husbands or mothers-in-law. They encouraged them to learn to read, speak at meetings, and to go to work.

In the new China no adult and few children were without an organization which overlooked the details of their political education. Women were members of neighbourhood committees or sometimes trade unions or special women's organizations. The teaching of the new organizations was that a woman's first duty was to be a good citizen. A ground for divorce was that one's husband or wife was a counter-revolutionary. Wives were expected to denounce husbands at struggle meetings, and to report suspicious conduct to government cadres. Failure to do so would involve the wife herself in accusations of counter-revolution. Young children had the same duties. Children's comics published strip features showing daring, resourceful children who had detected their parents in counter-revolutionary activity. In the final picture the children are being congratulated by the local officials, while the police lead the criminal parents away.

Partly for economic reasons, and partly for reasons of doctrinal equality, factories and offices have been encouraged to set-up nurseries and crèches. When the urban and rural communes were first formed it was stressed that the many new nurseries, and the communal dining halls, and facilities for washing and mending clothes would 'free' women. They would reach new stature when they were full citizens working outside their homes. But Western stories of the total abolition of ordinary married life, are mistatements. Husbands and wives, particularly if both were cadres, students or emigrants to a new industrial area, were sometimes housed in separate dormitories. But it was never a policy to separate ordinary established married couples in towns or villages. Where new flats and houses are built they are always designed for family units often including space for old parents.

Like the old-fashioned family the Christian churches offered a mental escape from the communist system. Their Western connexions and ministers encouraged Western ideals in their converts. They might even have become centres of anti-communist thought and perhaps action. Communist pressure was put on the churches, first of all to get rid of their foreign funds and foreign connexions. The Western missionaries were pressed to leave; and those who did not became the victims of sometimes fantastic accusations.

The all-Chinese churches were then expected to adapt themselves to the niche prepared for them in the new society. There was official religious toleration, and in many cases the government was generous over tax rebates and other financial concessions. In return the churches had to act as patriotic organizations, and form their own pressure groups to support new government policy. Most of the Protestant churches and their million members did not find this incompatible with Christianity. Their main complaint was that their members were illegally discriminated against by over-enthusiastic cadres and schoolteachers.

The three million Roman Catholics were in a more difficult position. Many of their priests thought that it was impossible for them to cut their connexion with the Vatican. But the communists found this continuing and direct link with a foreign power suspect. Roman Catholic churches and their organizations, particularly the Legion of Mary, were accused of harbouring spies and saboteurs. The Bishop of Shanghai, Monseigneur Ignatius Kung, was arrested, together with several hundred other Shanghai Catholics. The Vatican excommunicated those priests and lay Catholics who tried to make their peace with the new state, thus adding to communist suspicions. In the resulting uneasy compromise most Chinese Catholics ended neither trusted by the communists, nor in full communion with Rome.

Buddhism and Islam are more compatible with the new state. Buddhist temples and monks are on the whole left alone. But, like the Protestants, the Buddhists complain that their influence drops steadily among the young. The Moslems had the advantage of being most numerous in border areas where the communists are careful not to cross the feelings of non-Chinese people needlessly. Their foreign friends also are in countries China is anxious not to offend. Islam is not only tolerated, but in Sinkiang and in the north-west there were sometimes generous government grants for the repair of mosques, and to subsidize Mullahs' schools and training colleges.

Even after 70 years of decline many more Chinese were influenced by the Confucian system of ideas (even if they only accepted parts of it) than any foreign importations. The communists, of course, denied the universal validity of the Confucian system; and they were concerned to fit Confucius and Mencius into their Marxist place as products of their time and class. They themselves and what they wrote was 'feudal'. Much of it was explicitly condemned as incom-patible with the Marxist view of a good society. Confucius' concepts of the family and the social structure were explained as the ideology of a ruling class bent on the subjection of the 'people'. Mencius' view of history as 'now order, now chaos' was also singled out for particular condemnation as denying the existence of progress and the Marxist synthesis. But Confucius, as the teacher who had set once and for all the standards of proper behaviour, had been dis-placed long before 1949. The new government had only to give a final kick to some of the ideas they condemned most vigorously. Thereafter they could afford to resurrect Confucius and the classical books as historical phenomena: an interesting achievement of the Chinese people's great past. Since the mid-fifties new editions of the Confucian classics have been published in Peking, and Con-fucian scholars are allowed to continue their work and to teach.

The communist leaders, naturally more daring than their subordinates, used quotations from the classics in speeches and pamphlets as early as the 1930s and 40s. Liu Shao-chi quoted Mencius as well as the less condemned classics in an address pub-lished as *How to be a Good Communist*. But Liu's quotations, like the recent introductions and editorial notes in the new editions of the classics, are permissible only if they support the communist mes-sage. What Confucius or Mencius says is no longer true by its own virtue; it is true by virtue of its agreement with Marxism and Maoism.

To most Chinese townspeople disturbances during the reform of the churches were minor compared to the dislocation of government and business in 'the three anti' and 'five anti' campaigns of 1951 and 1952. The three antis were anti-bureaucracy, anti-waste, and anti-corruption in government offices. The chief sufferers in the campaign were the civil servants who had previously served the Kuomintang. But, as in later campaigns, any communist cadre against whom one of the current sins was proved was likely to be more severely punished than a non-party member. Government officials were kept locked in their offices, sleeping and eating there, until each of them had traced their working history back and proved that they had never been implicated in bribery or bad work. The better the office the more difficult this justification would be, as cadres were given percentages of the officials they were expected to bring to justice, and might themselves suffer if they failed to find their full quota of criminals.

The five antis of the campaign against businessmen were bribery, tax evasion, stealing government property, cheating on contracts, and stealing state secrets. As in the campaign of the three antis, there were genuine evils to be eradicated in the structure of Chinese business. But the campaign suffered, even more than the three antis did, from over-enthusiastic cadres, anxious to fulfill their quota of wrongdoers and ignorant of how complicated town government and business worked. 'Stealing state secrets' was interpreted to mean discovering government intentions by whatever means, however accidental or licit, and using that knowledge to make profits.

Businessmen were in any case an anomaly to many communists. Mao had said they were to be tolerated for a time in new China. But their background made them natural objects of suspicion to the less sophisticated cadre. Like the government officials, business-men were locked in their offices and exhorted to confess. When they asked what they were accused of, and what they should confess to, they were told to think and examine their account books. Special cadres called 'Tiger Beaters' were sent from office to office to rout out 'the tigers of bourgeois thought and action', bully the businessmen, and rouse their offices against them. Office managers were accused at public meetings by their workpeople; and, if they confessed humbly and if their sins were not too grave, they were sentenced to pay large fines. There were few executions; but those there were, were filmed, so that groups of recalcitrant businessmen could be shown what could happen to them. It was at this time that the grim joke circulated in Shanghai that it was unsafe to walk on the main streets because of the suicides plummeting from the upper office windows.

Later on the cadres' excesses particularly in the five anti campaigns were officially condemned. It was said that in the early campaigns against counter-revolutionaries some of the innocent had even been shot. But campaigns have continued: against the business community again; against corruption and bureaucracy in the Communist Party; against writers and those who had supported Hu Feng in his heresy that art could be separated from the interests of the state; against all intellectual and prominent critics of the Communist Party. Following all these campaigns there is tacit or open acknow-ledgement that the innocent have been punished, or that punishment has been over-severe. Accused people are allowed to slide back quietly into their old jobs. Cadres are reproved or sent elsewhere. Life is generally easier for most people for a few months. Then there is a new editorial in the Peking *People's Daily* denouncing a new group. It is copied in local newspapers. New directives are sent to local cadres, new meetings held, and a new campaign is under way.

The Chinese communists allege that these constant campaigns have been necessary. The pressure of revolutionary change must be kept up; and the roots of bourgeois thought must be dug out for the sake of the individual as well as for the health of society as a whole. Even more serious, they say, are the constant activities of saboteurs paid by the twin paper tigers of the Kuomintang in Taiwan and the American Imperialists in the West.

In Taiwan the Kuomintang do their best to add substance to communist claims by boasting of their continued war against the régime, and the activities of their guerrillas on the mainland. But the activities of all possible Kuomintang and American-trained saboteurs have to be stretched very thin indeed if they are to account for all the accusations of foreign-inspired counter-revolution.

An argument put forward by some critics of the communist government is that these constant claims of sabotage are caused by the Chinese leadership's paranoia. The Chinese leaders, so the argument goes, have been maddened, much as Stalin was in his last years, by the contradictions in their own doctrine and by unquestioned power. Because their doctrine must be faultless and they themselves are faultless in following it, state difficulties and disputes must come from outside enemies or from internal treachery.

However, the case for the Chinese leaders' paranoia or a comparison of them with Stalin is weak at several points. They have, in fact, not claimed to be faultless, although faults in policy and the execution of policy are generally blamed on cadres below the top ranks of the party. In marked contrast to what happened to the Russian leadership in the 1930s there have been no spectacular trials or accusations of treason among the heads of the Chinese Communist Party. On the few occasions when the top leadership has been seriously divided the split has been belittled, and has not been followed by any vendettas against the fallen leaders' personal followers.

In 1959 there were doubts among some of the top leaders about the policies of the Great Leap Forward (the rapid introduction of communes, and the forced pace of industrialization). Some of these doubts may have been communicated to the Russians. Among those who were involved were Chen Yun, who was senior deputy premier, and Marshal Peng Teh-huai, the then Minister of Defence, one of the most respected of the civil-war veterans, and the commander of the Chinese volunteers in Korea. Both men disappeared temporarily from public life. Chen Yun after a few months reappeared on state occasions in, apparently, positions of accustomed prestige. In 1965 he was again appointed deputy premier, but this time to rank second not first in their hierarchy.

Peng Teh-huai has not, at the date of writing, reappeared in public life (in 1960 he attended a colleague's funeral). In 1965 he was not re-elected as a deputy premier, but he has also not been publicly deprived of his party offices, his parliamentary membership or his defence council post (he was dismissed from the Ministry of Defence in 1959). His quarrel with official policy may have been as much about the army changes at the time of the Great Leap Forward as about strictly economic policy. Attempts to make the army more democratic, by having officers serve part of the time in the ranks, and to increase party control of the army were not popular among soldiers. There was also professional criticism of the arms given to the peasant militia instead of to the regular army, the cessation of military supplies from the Soviet Union, and the diversion of soldiers on to farm work. The Chinese communist leaders have always been particularly sensitive to the dangers of an army coup; or even an over-professional army attempting to manipulate policy so as to secure better military supplies and strategy. In the summer of 1965 military over-professionalism was again hit when all badges and titles of office were abolished in the Chinese army.

Neither the paranoia alleged against the Chinese leaders or their own allegations of sabotage are as convincing reasons for the continuing purges as the historical and psychological background of the Chinese people. There were national characteristics which made them initially welcome their particular brand of communist moral uplift; and national characteristics which seemed an unlikely foundation for a continuing communist state. Until 1911 the Chinese had been governed by emperors who not only told people what to do, but told them in terms of great moral superiority how they should behave and think.

People were used to being organized into small groups and letting officials know the details of their households. (The Mongols, after their conquest of Hangchow in the thirteenth century, had the names of the inmates posted on every house door.) Meetings to explain proper conduct and the politico-moral education of schoolchildren were familiar. The rebellious peasants of the Yellow Turbans in the second century A.D. had even encouraged the public confession of sins. Above all the idea that there is one, and only one correct line of conduct, is central to Chinese thought.

On the other hand many of the old traditions of Chinese family strength were inimical to any efficient modern government. The first loyalty of the good communist citizen, the communists had to emphasize, was to the state not to his family. It was illegal and improper to enrich one's family while robbing the state by bribery and corruption. They then added that it might be right to leave one's small children in a nursery or one's parents in an old people's home if the work one was then free to do was of national importance.

In the towns Chinese shopkeepers and craftsmen had developed one of the most competitive traditions in the world. Acute poverty made small differences in prices very important; and there were no effective restrictions on conditions, hours of work, or the quality of goods produced. Shopkeepers and businessmen were used to evading legislation designed to impress rather than to be universally enforced. They were used also to negotiating their own conditions with local and central governments, and to buying or by-passing the official sanctions needed.

Westerners who knew China in the 1920s and 1930s called the Chinese the most individualist people in the world. Many of these Westerners have been quite unable to accept that the new government in which individualism is a major sin, stays in power by anything except the most rigid repression of the majority of the people. (Their view is important, because some of 'the old China hands' with this background are now advisers on Chinese affairs to Western institutions and governments. More of them, ex-businessmen largely from Shanghai, work in Hongkong where their advice is freely given to those reporting or visiting communist China.)

The evidence commonly quoted to show that many of the Chinese people are opposed to their government is the outburst of the Hundred Flowers Movement in 1957.[31] This remarkable episode followed the post-Stalin thaw in the Soviet Union. Mao Tse-tung made a speech to communist leaders, and extracts from it were then leaked to the Chinese public. The most picturesque quotations referred back to the Golden Age of Chinese philosophy: 'let a hundred flowers blossom, let a hundred schools of thought contend'. It was interpreted as an invitation to criticize government policies; and after an initial hesitation the criticisms mounted to fill every newspaper, notice board, and discussion meeting in the country. Those who were backward with their criticisms were told that it was unpatriotic and uncommunist not to speak out now.

There were complaints about living conditions and bureaucracy from town workers. But the bulk of the Hundred Flowers criticisms were from businessmen, politicians outside the Communist Party, and people who in the West would be classed as holding professional jobs. Most of the criticisms were about communist privileges, methods and personnel rather than about the basic aims and existence of the communist state. A constant note in the complaints was that Communist Party officials were arrogant, or usurped all power for themselves and other members of the party in contrast to the principles they professed. 'Feudal princes and stinking charlatans,' said one professor complaining about communist officials in the university administration.

Most of the universities copied Peking's 'Democratic Wall' on which were pinned critical notices, and student meetings fanned the mounting excitement. Krushchev's speech denouncing Stalin, which had been kept secret in China, was first published by Peking University; and students drew dangerous morals. The more extreme statements were not published until after the Hundred Flowers Movement had been officially ended, and the process of 'pruning the dangerous weeds' had begun. The rightists of the Peking Geological Institute were then reported to have called for the killing of all Communist Party members; and at Nankai University the slogan 'Exterminate the Communist Bandits', was published and Mao's writings condemned as designed to mislead the people. At Hanyang the senior schoolchildren rioted, ransacked educational offices, and took unpopular cadres prisoner.

It has been said that the more extreme student statements were invented by the government after the Hundred Flowers Movement to enlist popular support for the suppression of the critics. This suppression was carried out by confessions, self-criticisms, public condemnations, and sometimes the exile or demotion of those concerned. The only executions reported were those of three of the leaders of the Hanyang school riot. Undoubtedly the Communist

Party leaders took a serious view of their unpopularity with at least a section of the student population. They blamed the bourgeois background of the rightist students; but even the students from the most bourgeois backgrounds had had eight years of communist schooling, classes in Marxism, and meetings to denounce the sins of their parents. They were, moreover, as students a privileged and selected class. Student food and dormitories seemed drab to Western visitors, but they were better fed, housed and clothed than the majority of the population. One of the results of the Hundred Flowers was that the party leadership apparently decided that students were over-privileged, and over-separated from the trials of the rest of the population. There was new stress on 'learning through labour'. Students were expected to spend longer periods during their vacations, and immediately they graduated, on manual labour, generally in village communes. Half-work half-study schools became an increasingly important part of the educational system. In May 1965 the Peking *People's Daily* stated in an editorial that: 'the system of study combined with factory or farm work will remove an important breeding ground for the restoration of capitalism.'

An argument about China is whether the Hundred Flowers Movement represented a basic and general discontent with the communist government; a discontent that was only just showing its full extent when the campaign ended; or whether it showed a more surface discontent with bureaucracy, some specific complaints, and the general excitability and idealism of all students. How far has this discontent, whether on the surface or deeper, survived the renewed political thought moulding which followed the campaign? Does it still exist in much the same forms today?

Most visitors to China now receive the impression of a united and indoctrinated country. No one, or scarcely anyone, complains openly to them. Many of these visitors are anyway well disposed towards communism. The sort of Chinese they come into contact with are, indeed, likely to be firm supporters of the government: interpreters or the chairman of village communes, or presidents of women's associations – official spokesmen of all kinds. Discontent would have to be officially approved, before they would voice it.

Popular unrest, however, beyond a certain point would be difficult to hide, and lead to rebellion. Diplomats, visiting businessmen, even the evidence of Chinese refugees in Hongkong agree that rebellion is very unlikely. Most of what they say supports the view that only a minority of Chinese are still hostile to communism; and only a very small number would prefer the present alternative government of the Kuomintang.

58 'Make our economy prosperous' reads a communist poster of the 1950s; this was one of the primary aims of the new communist government and a principle of the People's Democratic Dictatorship.

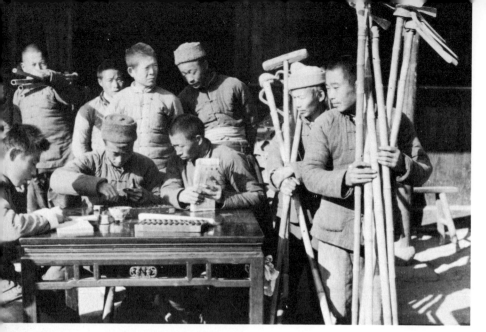

59 Land reform in China was confiscation of land from the landlords and its re-distribution among the peasants. In this photograph new title deeds and farm imple-ments are being distributed.

60 These capitalist businessmen 'voluntarily' surrendered their enterprises to the state in 1956. Previously, however, there had been considerable economic and personal pressure on all capitalists by the communist régime.

61 In 1958 the year of the 'Great Leap Forward' People's Communes which aimed at collective farming were established. Harvesting at the Hochang People's Commune.

62 Traditional terraced cultivation continued on a massive scale. This is in the Barian Hills, Kwangsi-Chuang Autonomous Region.

63 Squalor and untidiness were repugnant to the cadres of the new régime who were sometimes over-zealous in their enthusiasm for cleanliness and good order.

64 Scrupulous cleanliness extended to daily sweeping of the roads. This is in 1960 in the suburbs of Peking.

65 Women cadres of the new régime encouraged all women to free themselves of their 'feudal shackles' and go out to work. This is a meeting of women dockers.

66 Women take a lead in encouraging cotton-growers to use progressive methods.

67 (*Above*) At a communist court this woman is trying to obtain a divorce. A ground for divorce is for one of the parties to be a counter-revolutionary.

68 (*Below left*) The régime insisted that the only way was that of communism; any expression of counter-revolutionary activity was suppressed by imprisonment. A communist political prison cell.

69 (*Right*) Roman Catholicism is officially tolerated by the new government; but only at the expense of Catholics severing their ties with Rome.

70 (*Far right*) Buddhism and Islam are more compatible with communism. This is at the Buddhist University in Peking.

71 (*Below right*) Peking Moslems celebrate the Bairam Festival.

72 The people have the right to vote for their Deputies who sit in the National People's Congress. This is at Anshan in 1950 where the list of Deputies is displayed.

73 The annual commemoration of Liberation is celebrated on 1 October. This display outside the National People's Congress in Peking represents the industrial output in 1959.

8   New Scholars and Artists

THE CHINESE TRADITION of the official who retired to his native province, because he disagreed with the policy of the government of the day, was at least as strong and as admired as the tradition of the protesting censor. By 1949 students had got used to rioting against government they disapproved of. Most of their elders, the class who had once been the emperor's scholar officials, had withdrawn in disgust from government. It was better, the scholars of the interregnum thought, not to risk one's own corruption or one's family's ruin by trying to clean out the Augean Stables of the administration. They retired mostly to the universities, but country estates or even Western business were preferable to the new civil service. They remembered, however, that as the educated and civilized men of their generation it was still the government's proper duty to listen to them; and their's to admonish and advise, even if not actively to commit themselves.

This superior withdrawal was as obnoxious to the communists as the students' rioting. No admonition, it was soon made clear, was possible or tolerable to those to whom absolute Marxist-Maoist truth had already been revealed. Anyone who retired to their native province would be expected to take part in productive work by joining the local agricultural co-operative, and submitting to the political education organized for them by the local cadre.

There has, however, been some re-thinking about advice from those outside the party. Very useful advice, tactfully wrapped up in Maoist language and designed to further the long-term ends of the revolution, has at times been acceptable from members of certain professions, even when they were not party members. Engineers,

133

and a few other specialists, in practical sciences have been allowed this liberty. But, during the early periods of political pressure even engineering advice was only acceptable from the politically pure, and the quoted slogan was about the need to be both 'red and expert'. Red first, but the order of importance was reversed when times got, politically, easier.

However, this was never a concession for the less immediately useful professions: artists, writers, university and school teachers, doctors, and most research scientists – the people who appeared to themselves, and to much of the rest of the world, as the direct custodians of the traditions of Chinese culture. The communist view of their proper place in the new society has always been clear. As early as 1942 Mao Tse-tung endorsed for China the classic Marxist subordination of art and literature to the interests of the proletariat. One of the best known of the authors then in Yenan, Ting Ling, criticized herself, and the editor who had published her articles, for adverse comments, not about the basic tenets of communism, but about the arrogance of party members. Young authors, dramatists, and artists in Yenan were instructed to concentrate on work showing party members and Red Army soldiers as flawless heroes, and exhorting people to further sacrifices on their behalf. The intellectuals were told to be 'educational and popular'. The audience they were to aim at were 'workers, peasants, soldiers and cadres'. (Some at least of their work had close parallels to articles in wartime Britain which were equally designed to increase public support for the war effort.)

In 1949 the pressure on the intellectuals was not at first heavy. They were encouraged to visit the villages, watch the peasants rejoice in their new landholdings, and hear about their grievances against the landlords. Like the rest of the population they went to meetings, and were expected to master Marxist doctrine.

All artists, however, became members of a big union: the All-China Federation of Literary and Art Circles. This Federation has nine branches: literature, drama, painting, music, dance, folk arts, vocal music, films, and photography. Between them the Federation and its branches control teaching institutes for the arts, studios, theatres, and most outlets for book and picture publication. If an artist wants his work to appear it is only sensible for him to follow any suggestions the Federation makes about themes or alterations. In return the recognized members of these unions found that they were guaranteed regular salaries even if considerable time passed during which they did not produce new work. Writers received about £15-£30 ($42-$84) a month in 1964, less than an engineer but more than most skilled workers. They also received small fees on each printing of their books: the author of a best seller makes £1,000-£2,000 ($2,800-$5,600) from it. Successful Chinese writers are nowhere near as financially well-off as Russian writers.

In 1954, in the first ideological thaw following Stalin's death, a literary critic, Hu Feng, published a long justification of the idealist position in literature. His article was heavily attacked as 'subjective'; supporting the writers' withdrawal into 'Ivory Towers', instead of their immersion in the life and problems of peasants and workers. The literary attacks on him were reinforced by accusations of sabotage, and past and present intrigues with the Kuomintang.

Meanwhile Hu Feng's article and his crimes had been made the occasion for a tightening of controls over intellectuals generally, and over writers particularly. Countrywide meetings were called at which intellectuals were expected to criticize not only Hu Feng's views, but also what they themselves had said in the past which might be construed as 'subjective thinking'.

Once again the pressure slackened, this time culminating in the Hundred Flowers Movement. Throughout the country intellectuals voiced their discontent with heavy-handed party control, not only of what they wrote or the research they did, but also of what they read. All Western books and the ideas in them, they complained, had been automatically bad, all Russian ones good.

In the reaction from the Hundred Flowers Movement, the mass recanting of the rightists whose criticism had been too outspoken, and the punishment among others, of Ting Ling, many of the old rules about what could be written, painted, produced, read, or said, were re-introduced, but not with quite the same fervour as in the mid-fifties. Another period of relaxation followed. Most of the rightists (but not Ting Ling), were allowed to slip back into their old employment. Once again there was limited freedom of work, and, after the Sino-Soviet breach, Western learned periodicals and books were more freely available. Then, in the autumn of 1964, an article in *Red Flag* called for renewed class struggle. Creative writers particularly were rebuked for their frivolity. The example was quoted to all intellectuals of the amateur workers and peasants who painted, wrote film scenarios, novels or poems in their spare time. Group writing, under the leadership of local Communist Party Committees, was noted with particular approval as likely to be doctrinally pure and correct.

Yet whatever doubts they might have about Marxism, most Chinese intellectuals supported the government's new political nationalism: its independence of foreigners, and its reassertion of China's traditional place in the world. Cultural nationalism, however, was less acceptable. They had been warned about it. Just as the Marxist limits on intellectuals had been defined at Yenan, so had the nationalist. They must work, they were told at Yenan, within 'national' forms and use 'national styles'. Later on communists, throughout China used the slogan 'walk on two legs'. It was a useful multipurpose slogan. It could mean the combination of industry with agriculture (communes and rural factories); but it was also used to stress the combination of Chinese and Western traditions of learning.

For a time there was see-sawing with the emphasis sometimes on Western learning, sometimes on the Chinese heritage. After the break with Russia, however, the see-saw came decisively down on the side of national tradition because there was now no doctrinally pure source of Western expertise. Nationalism appeared in unexpected places. In 1964 it was revealed with horror that in the National Orchestra 70 per cent of the musicians played instruments of foreign, Western origin. The orchestra was reformed so that Chinese instruments predominated. But the orchestra continued to have, as the major part of its repertoire, stirring marches and accompaniments to patriotic songs which sounded closer to the international brass band than to Chinese tradition.

The results on Chinese civilization of the restraints of Marxism and nationalism were very variable. The Chinese intellectuals were fortunate that nationalism did stop the wholesale adoption of every-thing in the communist West. On the other hand, the need to learn Marxism and the stress, at first, on learning from Russian experience, broke some of the old rigid Chinese cultural patterns, and, parti-cularly in specialized scientific fields, stimulated new research.

No field of Chinese culture has been so disputed over as medicine. The first Western doctors to practise in China despised traditional medicine, and they taught their Chinese students that it was little but quackery. Some of the drugs of the traditional pharmacopoeia, however, notably ephedrine from the Chinese Ma-Huang, had been known and valued in the West for many years.

What seemed pure black magic to most Westerners were Chinese methods of treatment, particularly acupuncture and the theories of anatomy and psychology on which it was founded. In acupuncture hot, cold, or, nowadays, electrically stimulated, needles are stuck into the body at various key points generally far from the site of the pain. Cirrhosis of the liver is classically treated by a needle stuck an inch or so into the flesh just below the knee. The theory is that the internal organs and the external parts of the body are connected by twelve channels, most of which are unknown in Western medicine.

Psychologically, traditional Chinese medical practitioners lay great stress on tailoring their medical prescriptions to the needs of the individual. Illness, they say, is caused by a disturbance of the natural balance. But this balance is different for different people. To treat somebody successfully traditional doctors have to know about their family relationships, where they come from, what worries them, and, in the present society, their doctrinal and class background. In the course of treatment psychological, as well as physical disturbances, should be healed.

Acupuncture is not painful. Even when needles are pushed with some force far into the flesh, all that the patient feels is what is generally described as 'a gathering sensation'. It is very suitable for outpatient work. Its practitioners will treat anything from brain tumours to appendicitis, and there is no need for expensive surgical techniques. Besides its cheapness, the drugs and instruments needed for traditional medicine are easily available in China, and there are many more of its practitioners already at work than there are Western doctors. Doctrinally Chinese medicine complies with the communist argument about 'the wisdom of the masses'. Many Chinese, particularly the older peasants, prefer traditional to Western medicine.

Since 1949 traditional medicine has achieved a new respectability among the educated Chinese. New hospitals have been established devoted entirely to Chinese medicine, and some of the best town hospitals are mixed, offering both Western and traditional treatment. The Chinese naturally claim good results from traditional medicine; and its failures (like the official advocacy of live tadpoles swallowed after intercourse as a contraceptive) have been conveniently buried. Most Westerners are doubtful about the efficacy of widespread use of acupuncture. But, even the doubtful, like Western journalists, when they try acupuncture in China for ailments like colds or indigestion, often claim to have had some benefit from it; and it seems to work better than most other known treatments for rheumatism. At present there are clinics of acupuncture in the Soviet Union and in France, and several qualified specialists in its use in London.

In the meantime there have been indisputable advances in Western medicine in China. By 1959 nearly 50,000 fully qualified doctors had been trained, and four times that number of partially trained medical auxiliaries. The campaign for cleanliness, the building of new hospitals and new country clinics, mass vaccinations and inoculations, and new housing in cities with lavatories linked to efficient town sewage systems, have greatly raised Chinese health standards. Childbirth and the care of small children has been one of the priorities for medical help, and infant and maternal mortality has fallen dramatically.

At the time of the Hundred Flowers Movement there were relatively few complaints about medicine: except the universal one of bureaucratic Communist Party meddling. The only mistake constantly alleged against the responsible ministries was too great reliance on Soviet methods. Russian doctors taught their methods of 'painless childbirth'; and preached, doctrinally so effectively, that in the Peking hospitals women were referred to as having a 'painless but sore parturition'.

Concerning the other sciences Professor Mikhail Klochko, one of the visiting Soviet experts, has published a somewhat discouraging report.[32] Professor Klochko, who is a chemist, found competent senior scientists, promising juniors, and reasonably well-equipped and spacious laboratories in the institutes he visited. But there was doctrinaire control of scientific projects, inadequate graduate training, too much research secrecy (in Kunming he found a girl working on a problem already solved in a Peking laboratory), and above all scientists' time was wasted on endless political meetings. He visited laboratories which, during working hours, were denuded of all responsible scientific staff. He also found that the higher the grade of the scientist the more meetings he had to attend and the less time he had for research.

Professor Klochko visited China during the Great Leap Forward and its aftermath. It was a time of particular political pressure on Chinese intellectuals. Two years later when conditions in China were generally easier and more relaxed, the Royal Society delegation reported in more optimistic terms. Like Professor Klochko they found laboratory standards varied greatly. But, in the opinion of most of them, senior scientists were not unduly worried by political pressures and time wasted on meetings. In the main laboratories they found research work of a high standard on both 'pure' and applied subjects.

The high standard of Chinese physics, anyway, is supported by the evidence of the Chinese atomic bombs, made without Russian help. Nuclear physicists are said to be subjected to less political harassment than other Chinese; and their work is helped by the pressure on students to specialize in the physical rather than the biological sciences.

Building, and the decoration of buildings, was one of the traditional glories of China. But when the communists took power it had become a neglected glory. In Peking, in the Forbidden City, just before 1949, weeds were growing in the imperial courtyards, rubbish piled up in pavilions, walls were falling down, roofs were falling in, and nothing was painted or swept. The new government had an immediate spring clean. The palace was meticulously restored on the advice of historians and architects. The pillars of the great pavilions were gilded and re-lacquered in colours to match pictures of their original painting. The marble balustrades were re-carved, and golden coloured tiles baked for the roofs.

There was a similar reconstruction of temples and palaces outside Peking. The palaces at Sian, the lakeside pavilion at Hangchow, even the monstrous nationalist monuments to Sun Yat-sen at Canton, were tidied, repaired, and used for appropriate displays. At Hangchow they even replaced the carp the Kuomintang had killed in one of the temple pools.

New town planning and the new buildings, particularly those built in Peking, have been less successful. Under the emperors the great gates and the Imperial palace dominated the city's small grey houses and narrow streets. The imperial prohibition on buildings able to overlook the palace was little breached by the Kuomintang, partly because their capital and therefore most of their new building was at Nanking. But the communists moved the capital back to Peking. New main roads, considerably larger than the amount of traffic yet makes necessary, were driven through the old complex of lanes; and large blocks of offices, new flats and hotels were built, overshadowing the old palace and walls.

To begin with much of the detail of several of the new Peking buildings were modelled on the old imperial palaces. Their roofs were curved up in the way the emperors had hoped would cheat the stupider flying devils who could only manage straight lines. The roof tiles had to be specially baked, and sometimes offices and hotels had porches or halls of carved and lacquered pillars. These buildings were expensive, and during the mid-fifties increasingly condemned as extravagant and tasteless. Newer buildings were starker, but still often ornamented with statues and pillared entrances. The style was similar to that adopted for Stalin's new buildings in Moscow, and throughout the communist world. Many foreigners and some Chinese have regretted the changing of old Peking, and the absence of any new local style in the building of the new city.

There have also been doubts in China, although of a rather different sort, about the restoration of the old palaces and their use to display the imperial collections. The buildings had undoubtedly been used for 'feudal' and 'imperialist' purposes. A young Intourist guide told me that it was for these reasons that she did not like showing foreigners round them. She thought they gave 'a wrong impression of modern China'.

This girl, a Shanghai college graduate in her early twenties, had also reluctantly followed me round an exhibition of early paintings from the Imperial collections. Most of them were of court scenes: imperial children at play, an empress embroidering surrounded by her maid-servants, an emperor hunting.

'These pictures,' the girl said, 'are not interesting to me. They do not teach any moral lesson.' She preferred, she said, an exhibition of Russian paintings which had recently toured China. They were in the Socialist Realist (or Pre-Raphaelite) style: a young Pioneer rebuking his drunken grandfather; heroic portraits of Stakhanovites; two girls leaning eagerly out of the window of a model village house when the soldier's letter arrives from the front.

The classic Chinese tradition of painting and the classic communist one have in fact co-existed since 1949. Traditional Chinese ink and brush-work scrolls of great beauty and delicacy are still being painted in China by men tolerated by the state and even state-subsidized. Subjects are classic: lotus and plum blossom, willows, wild geese, cormorants, boats, mountains, waterfalls and lakes. Fu Pao-shih, one of the most admired artists in China today, in 1962 painted a picture he called 'Sitting Beside the Tai Lake After Playing the Ku Chin'. The painting, like the musical instrument it refers to, has a Sung dynasty ancestry. Its subject is one of the classic formulae – lapping water and mist with on the hill above one solitary white-robed figure. Fu Pao-shih has students and colleagues who follow the same austere and scholarly tradition of the classic imperial

painters. But even they are expected always to keep political considerations in mind. One of the other pictures Fu Pao-shih exhibited in
1962 was called 'The Yellow River Runs Clear', and was officially
pointed out as evidence of the artist's admiration for the achievements
of the state and the river control workers.

The Chinese paintings, however, which are easiest for most
Westerners to like and understand are livelier and more frivolous.
The men painting them are successors, the Chinese say, to the icono-
clast, and often politically revolutionary, artists of the eighteenth
century. Chi Pai-shih until his death in 1957 was a painter in this
tradition whose works figured largely in every exhibition for
foreigners. He ran a studio of artists painting all the types of pictures
he had made famous, mostly small animals and flowers, and in
his last years the master did little more than add an approving
blossom to a picture he liked, or a pair of bees, or a laudatory
inscription. A younger man in the same popular style is Li Ko-jan
whose buffaloes and cheerful southern children have been extensively reproduced.

The more austere traditional Chinese paintings, with their
economy of line and sentiment, have been greatly admired by some
Western abstract painters. Li K'u-ch'an's eagle or Wu Tso-jen's
camel caravan are very close to modern Western painting. Wu
Tso-jen studied in Europe, and he has been particularly drawn to
the spaces of China's far north and west rather than to crowded,
traditional, mountain and water landscapes. But modern Western
painting, even non-abstracts, is condemned in China. Very few of
the paintings in an exhibition of modern British art taken to China
were much liked by the people who saw them or by the artists
charged with their official criticism. Abstracts and many of the other
paintings were 'decadent'. The Chinese particularly disliked the
Western use of yellows and greens. 'The colours of a decaying
corpse', one of them said about a still life.

The exhibitors had wondered whether 'kitchen sink' paintings
would be popular. They had included a portrait of a miner in his
home, and a working-class kitchen interior. But the kitchens, the
Chinese said, were untidy and squalid. The miner looked small,

overwhelmed, and tired. These pictures were, if anything, more disapproved of than the abstracts. The worker heroes of Chinese pictures (like the many portraits of Mao Tse-tung himself) are expected to be larger than life, confident, perhaps smiling, and posed against a perfect field of corn or a smoothly running, tidy and modern factory.

In accordance with the dictum of the Yenan Forum artists paint for the people, and to further their cause; so the sort of subject commonly chosen will be 'Girls Bringing in the Commune's First Harvest', 'An Old Woman (but not a toothless or ugly old woman) Learns to Read', or 'The First Steel Ingot is Forged'. Among the Western style paintings those with most originality are likely to be the landscapes and portraits of the great epic – the Long March.

It is perhaps unlikely that the two traditions of painting will survive for ever running parallel but entirely separate courses. At one period it looked as if traditional painting was considered second best except for its power as a foreign money-getter. In the Peking Central Institute of the Fine Arts, in the mid-fifties, all the paintings on the walls were of the Socialist Realist school. The Director reluctantly acknowledged to me that he did have Chinese traditional painters on his staff; but, he said, the students (like my interpreter) were 'not interested' in their work.

At the time of the Hundred Flowers Movement several well-known traditional-style painters complained of the neglect of their art, and the contempt with which students and teachers of the new style treated them. But since 1960 and the break with the Soviet Union, visitors' accounts suggest that there has been more emphasis on the importance of both historical and new, traditional-style paintings. One third of the paintings in the 1962 national art exhibition in Peking were officially described as 'traditional'; and the exhibition was accompanied by publicity about the studios of traditional artists and the training of their successors.

The Yenan precept about artists learning from the people has resulted in the official adoption and fostering of some arts which were previously confined to peasant amateurs. One of the pleasantest of these are the red and multi-coloured paper cutouts which peasant women make to stick on windows and doors at the New Year. The women base their ideas on a mixture of traditional design, local news, and what they think would be funny or suitable for the time of year. They have now been organized in commune work teams, and are sometimes provided with patterns. Their work is bought from them for general sale in China and abroad. The new designs for these cutouts have on the whole been agreeable; and the heroic subjects not too intimidatingly inhuman. Cheerful young women with corn sheaves, even a squarish version of Chairman Mao, fit well into the traditional patterns.

More sophisticated decorative art has suffered in much the same way as painting has done. Many craftsmen have been organized into co-operatives and emphasis has been placed on their political education. Bourgeois art-forms, they are told, should be avoided, and all should work for the good of the state. Classic pottery, silk hangings, carved ivory and jade are still produced, much of it for sale abroad. But there is less of a living tradition than with painting, and even less independence of thought among the designers for the crafts.[33] Much of the craftwork is debased, although still painstaking, partly because so much of it was aimed at the Soviet market. Soviet buyers admire lavishness and colour, and the Soviet technicians in China and their wives shopped for the usual sort of souvenir. Silver and gilt dragons embroidered on black silk were particularly popular, so was ivory and jade carved into ornate ashtrays.

In literature, as in art, there was the same difference between the traditional forms and the new 'educational' poems, novels, plays, and operas. The political direction of poetry developed complications because Mao Tse-tung's own poetry was written in the most allusive and compressed, classic Chinese style. The Foreign Languages Press' official translation of his poem on Loushan Pass reads:

Cold is the west wind;
Far in the frosty air the wild geese call in the morning moonlight.
In the morning moonlight,

the clatter of horses' hooves ring sharp,
and the bugle's note is muted.
Do not say that the strong pass is guarded with iron.
This very day in one step we shall pass its summit
We shall pass its summit!
There the hills are blue like the sea,
and dying sun like blood.

It is true that Loushan Pass was one of the strategic positions of the Long March, as explained by the official press in a footnote. The poem is, however, written in the classical *Tz'u* metre perfected in the Sung dynasty. When his poems were published in 1957 Mao suggested that this metre was unsuitable for young poets because 'these forms would cramp their thought and are difficult to master'. More straightforward metres and a more straightforward approach to their subjects were recommended to the young. Some of the results were translated in 1961 in *Songs of the Red Flag*:

> *I am past sixty but I can still work,*
> *And I find it as easy as when I was young.*
> *It's not that I am boasting about my strength,*
> *but here in my heart I have Mao Tse-tung.*

The vote of thanks customary to Mao and the leadership of the Communist Party is not always easy to work happily into songs or more seriously intentioned poetry. The government is, predictably, not particularly sympathetic to complaints of technical difficulty or the need for the right mood or right inspiration. There are poetry drives for a higher output of poetry, just as there are drives for higher agricultural and industrial output. (During the Great Leap Forward cadres boasted that Szechuan had produced a million new verses.)

The new poetry, conforming with the Yenan formulae, is expected to excite enthusiasm for the current official drive, describe in orthodoxly flattering terms the peasants or workers lives and achievements, and 'learn from the people' by imitating peasant verse.

Some of the poetry, however, produced under these conditions translates well, and has been received with genuine pleasure by Chinese outside communist control. The poets are helped by the similarity of most of the metres used in peasant verse to the classical forms. They use allusions to peasant myth and magic instead of the less approved classical allusions; and, as the more distant emperors of the Chinese heroic past are rehabilitated, references to their lives have become as acceptable in the new poetry as in the old. The correct moral is now, often rather loosely, attached in a couplet tacked to the end of a poem. Otherwise the poems are very like those written by Chinese outside China. In 1962 four poems by Ko Pi-chou were published. The first ends:

> New forest grows all round the Hill of Shou-Yang,
> Water below the dam of the Golden Valley is swelling, flowing,
> Behold where are the ruins of old Loyang city?
> I see only clouds and water, and oceans of trees densely without limit.
> The old dies, new life is born – life, life, never to end,
> Today the evening glory of the nimbus – tomorrow, the morning sun.[34]

Novels, at any rate in translation, have been less successful under the communists. Like the paintings of the Socialist Realist artists the most popular recent novels have a strong family resemblance to English Victorian literature. The strength of communist conviction has to be substituted for the strength of Christian conviction; but there is the same purposefulness working itself out through the same complicated plot, and at much the same (by Western standards), inordinate length. In the novels of the English Victorian writer, Miss C. M. Yonge, it would be useless to expect to find a bad sailor or a good Guards' officer. Similarly, in the successful Chinese novels, landlords and Kuomintang officials are always bad; poor peasants, industrial workers, and, above all, communist cadres are always good. Instead of defeating the school bully, a classical prize at Oxford, and ordination; the typical Chinese hero has defied the local wicked landlord, fought the Japanese, and unearthed a counter-revolutionary agent. His girl friend is at least as pure as her Victorian counterpart. Engaged couples in modern Chinese (and in Victorian) fiction do not touch. They gaze into each other's eyes

146

and talk about ethical doubts (Victorian) or increased production (Chinese) – agricultural or industrial, not, of course, human.

Most Victorian novelists were, however, able to allow more latitude to their characters than their Chinese counterparts. Mao Tun, the then Minister of Culture and Chairman of the Writers' Union, told the All-China Federation of Literary and Art Circles in 1960 that 'signs of weakness in a hero going to his death are intolerable distortions of a hero's character and not a matter of human interest at all'. The author of *Let Life Become More Beautiful* was severely reprimanded because his flirtatious heroine induced her village friends to volunteer for the army when the local cadres had failed to find new soldiers. The author was imputing improper motives to soldiers, who elsewhere are correctly shown worrying about their overdue Party subscriptions, or crawling with hideous wounds and important despatches upheld by the inspiration of Mao and the Communist Party.[35]

Both the government and the novelists, however, deplore the dullness of the work that these pressures produce. During the Hundred Flowers Movement Liu Shao-tang, writing about the mechanical situations and characters the official guide lines had produced, asked: 'Do we mean that in writing about peasants we can only use the following type of subject matter: Ahem! Ahem! Ahem! Let's exert ourselves and work with renewed vigour, so that the produce will be an inch taller?' Some of the work produced during the Hundred Flowers Movement was freer and more interesting than anything that had preceded it since 1949. But this overfree writing was soon censored. The answer to Liu Shao-tang became again that that was indeed the only permitted form of dialogue; and as yet neither the government nor the novelists had found a way of presenting it with much novelty or excitement.

Opera was by far the most popular branch of the arts in pre-communist China. Small clay medallions of the famous actors are collected by Chinese young people with something of the same adoration as pop singers rouse in the West. ('Yellow' pop music is far more stringently outlawed, as decadent and degrading, in China than in the Soviet Union. The young are officially encouraged to dance: preferably peasant rounds, but, if not these, approved waltzes like the Blue Danube. Boy generally dances with boy, and girl with girl, or if the sexes mix, they hold each other at arm's length.) Popular actors in the Peking opera are paid the highest salaries in China: about twice what a factory manager or engineer is paid, five times a civil servant's pay, and eight or ten times a factory worker's.

There are different local branches of opera in China with different traditions of dress, singing, and acting. Opera, like that of the Shanghai school, which in the old days was considered crude though popular, has received heavy state subsidies and a general lift in its prestige. But the most elaborately staged and dressed opera, that of Peking, is performed by Chinese troupes abroad and is highly esteemed by educated Chinese. Many of its conventions date back several centuries. The actors wear Manchu court dress. Their characters are drawn on their face with make-up so that the red stripes on the hero's chin proclaim him before he has opened his mouth. Men act women's parts. There is little scenery or stage properties, and the themes are taken from Chinese history or myth.

As with classical painting there were early suggestions from the young communists that traditional Peking opera was 'dull' and could be enlivened by modern stage conventions, costumes and stage properties. These suggestions were not, however, taken very seriously; and the conventions and costumes of the opera have been conserved with some minor alterations. Spitting is no longer allowed on stage. The blocks actors wore to symbolize the bound 'lotus feet' of well-brought up women have also been banned.

Opera themes, however, have been extensively reformed. There were even attempts to write entirely new plays for Peking opera, but the new plays never became popular. As part of the 'walking on two legs' policy the Peking opera actors were allowed to cite the greater popularity of the old themes with traditional backgrounds as reasons for reviving them. Some operas, however, were drastically re-written. Faithful servants, over-subordinate wives, the glorification of emperors not in present favour, were all weeded out.

It has been easier to write new plays for Shanghai opera where modern dress and modern themes had been customary before the revolution. Operas with titles like *The Wanton Woman Repines* and *The Amorous Lady Thief*, were replaced by *Reunion*, *The Life of a Peddicab Driver in the New Society*, and *It Can Be Done*, officially described as about a 'primary-school teacher's patient work with a backward child who has a discipline problem'.

In several of the arts the most successful of the models has been inspired by the revolutionary wars before the communists finally gained power. One of the most exciting new films (and a new opera) was based on the legend of the 'White-Haired Girl'. She fled from the cruel landlord's family, hid in a cave in the mountains, raiding the village temple for food. Her hair turned white, and only with the return to the village of the Red Army could she come out, singing her woes, and calling for vengeance.

So far operas and films – and pictures, poems, and novels – about the successful communists have lacked the imaginative drive and excitement of those about their struggle for power. The communists maintain, with some reason, that the building of the new society should be as exciting as the revolutionary wars. However, up until now the rules they impose about character and subject matter have made it impossible for artists to capture this excitement.

9   Building Perfection

FOR MANY YEARS the great Western myth about the Chinese
communists was that they were 'nothing but agrarian reformers'.
It owed much of its currency to the Western observers accompanying
the communist armies in Yenan during their days of anti-Japanese
compromise, conciliation, and moderation. But its origins went
back to the disputes among the Communist Party leaders in the
1930s, the victory of Mao's policy of moderation, and his reliance on
peasants for his army recruits, party members, and popular support.

Mao recognized peasant backing as essential for the first stage of
the revolution; but he never departed so far from Marxist orthodoxy
as to fail to acknowledge 'the advanced thinking' of the industrial
workers, and the part they had to play in the later stages of the
struggle towards communism. After the communists left Yenan,
there was a drive to recruit industrial workers, and, later, intellectuals
into the Communist Party. In the mid-sixties out of a total party
membership of 18 million, a third were of non-peasant origin.[36]

The perfect Chinese communist society was thus never planned,
except by Western wishful thinking, to be one of small independent
peasant proprietors living according to their ancient ways in a
country traditionally without heavy industry. On the contrary the
ultimate aim of the Chinese leaders was to make every Chinese a
worker. There were to be no more capitalists, no more bourgeois
intellectuals, and, in a way, no more peasants. Since China was
to be a modern country, capable of taking her rightful place as the
leader of the world, many of her citizens would be workers in new
heavy or skilled industries. Others would be worker-directors or
worker-intellectuals. On the land the former peasants would work
partly in rural factories. Even when they were farming their methods

and hours would be as regulated and methodical as if they were working in a factory.

In this utopia there would be no need for money. With everyone working there would be enough for everyone's needs. Personal greed and selfishness would be banished. With workers directing their own work, and managers and intellectuals also working with their hands, as well as with their minds, the evils of status and bureaucracy would go. It would be the perfect, the true communist society realized on earth; and it would be universally copied. Once more China would give civilization to the known world.

The Chinese tragedy of the moment is that for a short time the leaders were within touching distance of their ideal. At the height of the communes they talked about the realization here and now of communism in China. But the high dream failed. Recently Chou En-lai has insisted that China is only a socialist, not a communist, society.

Communism – perfection – has been the unconcealed aim of the leaders all along. But they thought it politically advisable to start with compromise. In Yenan even the landlords were tolerated. In China, as a whole, there was at first peace for everyone except landlords and bureaucratic capitalists.

As a start to socialism the new state had inherited from its predecessors certain businesses like the railways, the steel-mills and the coal-mines of the pre-revolutionary centre of heavy industry, Manchuria. The capitals of private enterprise were the coastal towns, particularly Shanghai and Tientsin. Here some industry and commerce came to the state by direct confiscation from the bureaucratic capitalists who had gone to Taiwan. Other firms were foreign owned. These were gradually squeezed out of business by large fines for breaches of the suddenly numerous new regulations, and also fines for breaches of the regulations under the Kuomintang.

The same sort of pressure was exerted on Chinese firms to become 'state-private' enterprises. In addition to financial difficulties Chinese directors were also liable to more direct personal persuasion through meetings they had to attend, and from their families. Their adolescent children, in several cases, decided it was their duty to denounce their fathers loudly and repeatedly in their offices before their embarrassed staff.

In state-private enterprises the state bought a certain share in the business. Generally the price paid was approximately the same as the firm's debts to the state. The state then took the profits from its share of the business, and the former owner from his share of the business. A state manager was put in and worked in uneasy collaboration with the old private directors and with the local Communist Party secretary. How much the state manager interfered depended on how much he knew about the technicalities of the business. Generally he was not expert in them.

The next step was for the private owners to agree to surrender their businesses altogether to the state. They were guaranteed seven to ten years interest on the capital invested in their business. Some of them were retained, on salaries, as technical advisers in their former factories or offices. A few years later there were reports that the former private owners had in many cases appealed to the state to surrender the remaining interest to be paid on their capital, so that they could be reclassified immediately as workers not capitalists. Nevertheless businessmen and former businessmen remained a relatively wealthy section of Chinese society. Some of them could afford to run large and luxurious households. The greatest pressure for social conformity and surrender of their capital was maintained on the smaller men, the least on those who had formerly been the most wealthy. In 1965 there were still a handful of millionaires left in Shanghai, ready to testify about their support of the communists to visiting Westerners.

On the whole the state made good use of its new possessions. In 1949 China was, compared to the West or to Japan, an unindustrialized country. In the next decade she went through a sizeable industrial revolution. Outputs of established industries, like the cotton spun in Shanghai or the steel produced at Anshan in Manchuria, climbed back to the level they had been at before the Japanese war. They then doubled and trebled. New sources of raw materials were found. China was short of oil and petroleum; and the new oil fields in the northwest, in Sinkiang and Tibet, were particularly important discoveries.

New factories were opened to make most of the world's known goods. Trucks and lorries came from the factory at Changchun; scientific instruments and machine tools from Harbin; and most products of light industry – plastics, bicycles, clocks, and fountain pens – from Shanghai. Some of the new factories were inefficiently run and workmen made elementary mistakes because they were unfamiliar with any machinery. The Changchun car-works, particularly, looked at one time more like a vast technical school, than a factory. But the teaching seems to have been efficient, and the factory's output and standards have both gone up.

Meanwhile the new government encouraged a strategically and economically healthier pattern of industrial development. The northwest, notably around Lanchow and Taiyuan, became an important new heavy manufacturing centre. It was closer to the new oil-fields than the old coastal industrial areas: close to coal, iron, and planned new hydro-electric development; and farther from the possibility of Western sea and air based attacks. But there were also smaller industrial centres – cotton-mills and light industry – set up all through the interior of the country from Canton to Inner Mongolia.

In contrast to the decline in working-class living standards during the European industrial revolution, the standards of most Chinese working people rose steadily during their country's rapid industrialization. In the Chinese industrial areas during the 1950s, people stopped dying on the streets from cold, hunger, or anything else. Wages, while low by European standards, were enough for a family to live decently, if both husband and wife worked; and the provision of nurseries and crèches made this generally possible. Safety regulations and rules about work conditions, although again below the minimum acceptable in Europe, were enforced and by Asian standards were reasonable. All over the industrial areas new government housing blocks are going up fast. They are drab looking, providing no more than one or two rooms for a family, with communal kitchens and bathrooms. They are, however, an improvement on the tin and sacking shacks of the past.

It is a constant sport for foreign journalists, touring these blocks, to try and pick a room where they are not expected. But even the families most surprised by the sudden incursion of a large party of journalists, interpreter and officials appear to be living with a modicum of furniture, blankets, clothes, and crockery. By Asian standards, again, the families are comfortable and well-housed.

Most visitors acknowledge that industrial workers and towns-people generally are better-off under the new government. But what is often said is that the towns are living off the country; and their relatively high standards are maintained at the expense of increasing poverty among the four out of five Chinese who live in villages.

In the villages, after the landlords' holdings had been redistribu-ted, peasants were left for a few months to enjoy their individual holdings. There was, however, increasing emphasis on traditional co-operation. Before communism Chinese villagers had often built houses together, sowed or harvested co-operatively. This tradi-tion was formalized and strengthened in the 'Mutual Aid Teams' of families doing most farm work together. 'Magic mats to fly towards Socialism', said one of the English-language magazines of the time. Meanwhile the cadres and national newspapers publicized stories of the unfairness of all private landownership: poor peasants whose holdings, even after land reform, were too small to give them a living; or rich peasants buying up their neighbours' holdings to make themselves into a new class of landlords.

Around 1954, the exact date varied from one part of China to another, the first village co-operatives were set up. In these the peasants farmed collectively. Profits from the land were divided – part for the owners of the land in proportion to the amount they had put into the co-operative, part for those who had laboured on the land in proportion to the labour they had put in. Co-operatives also took into account a family's needs and its political good standing when the labour profits were distributed.

In 1955 and 1956 the Chinese said that 'the high tide of Socialism' had led to the grouping of almost all peasants into 'higher form co-operatives'. Western writers called them 'collectives'. Most of the collectives included two or more villages, and they were organized either on the basis of the old co-operatives, or from two or three Mutual Aid Teams if the village had not had co-operatives. The peasants continued, theoretically, to own the land they farmed collectively. But profits were distributed only on the basis of the amount of labour put in, not on the basis of land (or tools or animals) contributed to the collective. The peasants were also allowed to keep small garden plots for their own private cultivation, and to keep private hens and, sometimes, pigs. In theory the peasants were allowed to withdraw both from the co-operatives and the collectives if they so wished; but few even tried to exercise this right.

By 1956 and 1957 no collective any Westerner visited failed to quote figures of greatly increased production and higher living standards. Nationally, large surpluses were being saved, mainly from agriculture, for export and investment in industry. But the government claimed that the peasants' consumption of grain, cloth, and small luxuries like new basins and thermos flasks was also steadily rising.

The cadres and newspapers had been right in the early 1950s when they had preached the impossibility of living with any margin on the average plot of a Chinese farmer. After land reform this varied from a fraction of an acre in the crowded Shanghai and Canton deltas (where, however, market gardening was very profit-able), to 3 to 4 acres in the emptier lands of the north and west. The average was under 2½ acres (in contrast to a European small-holder's 20 or 30 acres). Inevitably on the minute Chinese holdings much land had to be wasted on paths and boundary ditches, and it was not feasible to use large tools.

The new village collectives were least successful in the south where the growing of rice on small hillside terraces had to be done by hand.[37] In the north, however, on the flatter land there the collectives were able to use ploughs which were quicker and more efficient than the old hand tools. The leaders of the collectives were encouraged to buy better seeds and fertilizers, and to raise money to pay for this by low interest state loans. Lecturers from state agricultural colleges were sent round the villages to explain new methods to the peasant leaders. Meanwhile schemes of irrigation, drainage, re-afforestation and the ploughing of former pasture brought more land into cultivation.

These benefits were quoted by the Chinese authorities when they were asked how the cadres had overcome the Chinese peasant's traditional reluctance to surrender land he had or could have owned. Chinese novels of the late 1950s show other pressures similar to those exerted against recalcitrant businessmen. Peasants who refused to join co-operatives were not imprisoned but they could not get the new loans, fertilizers or seeds. Their marketing became difficult. Neighbours who had formerly helped them in their work now refused.

After the peasant holdings had once been surrendered to the collectives there was comparatively little feeling in most villages against the formation of the communes: the next stage in farm organization. The first commune is said to have started in Loyang (Honan) in April 1958, and news of it spread spontaneously around the country. The formation of new communes was officially approved in August 1958. The communes were organizations of sometimes 100 or more villages; at one time 25,000 to 26,000 of them covered the whole of China. They had their own administra- tions whose duty it was to organize farmwork, commune schools, hospitals, dining-rooms, and entertainments. The communes were encouraged to set up their own rural factories, and commune mem- bers were expected to spend part of their time working in them, or on public works such as irrigation schemes or dams.

Members were paid partly in wages, and partly by the 'free supply' system, in which they obtained food, clothing, housing, and other necessities, according to their needs and without paying. In most communes wages under this system were naturally very small. The women members of the commune were expected to work much the same hours as the men, and communal dining rooms, crèches, and centres for household jobs, and clothes making and repairing, were set up. There were no private gardens in many of the com- munes – the members did not have time to cultivate them. But there was time everywhere for the new militia units where commune members were drilled and trained after their day's work.[38] Military words of command and drills were sometimes used even in the fields, where units of the commune labour force were marched out in formation shouldering their rakes and hoes like rifles.

The communes were an experiment on an enormous scale, and in the end they were not a success. It is still not clear why they were set up so quickly in the first place, without giving the government time to learn from initial mistakes. 'Popular enthusiasm', the communists say, and the order recognizing the communes in August 1958 stressed the importance of official support not lagging behind the will of the people. That way lay the political sin of 'tailism'.

All reports suggest that there was in China in the summer of 1958 a spirit of great excitement among numbers of people, official and otherwise. It was fed by every possible means; and used as the motive force for what was called 'The Great Leap Forward'. It was to be the Great Leap from socialism to communism. There would be no need for money or central authority in this new perfection. The communes were to be locally administered, and in them the necessities of life would be given, in the classic Marxist phrase, 'to each according to their needs'. In the communes, the peasants as well as being peasants, would be promoted to workers, preferably workers in heavy industry. In most of the communes, along with the factories for bicycle parts, textile mills and the like, steel furnaces were set up: 'backyard steel furnaces'. Sometimes there was one in every village. They were to use iron cooking pots, collected from village housewives who would no longer need them now that their families could be fed at the new communal dining halls.

Millions of people left the country to help the Great Leap Forward in the town. Urban communes were formed although they were never as universal as the country communes. But, in Peking and Canton particularly, small factories were organized and run by local women, together with communal dining rooms, crèches, and mending centres. It had to be the women, as their husbands were too busy. The Great Leap had meant overtime and increased 'norms' (standards of what should be produced in a working day) in most offices and factories. Everywhere people pledged themselves to produce 20, then 50, then 100 per cent more than they had produced the year before.

There were sober economic arguments for the Great Leap. Its leaders hoped that a few years' intensive work, powered by the enthusiasm of the movement, would free China from her perpetual economic embarrassment. This was, and is, an ever-growing population with ever-rising standards of living chasing dwindling industrial and agricultural surpluses. One way out of the Chinese economic problem was for industrialization to be more rapid and thorough than it was being. For this a greater national investment was needed in industry, and it could only come from greater agricultural profits. By overtime for men, freeing women for work outside their homes, and organizing all labour on as large a scale as possible, the Chinese hoped to have enough manpower, not only to increase the production of existing farms and factories, but also to build enough dams, irrigation works, and canals, to make it possible to set up new and more efficient farms and new factories.

With all the enthusiasm behind it, and the efforts and overwork of the Chinese, the Great Leap slipped. A part of the difficulties was sheer bad luck. 1959, 1960, and 1961 were years of natural disaster: drought in the north, floods in the south, and typhoons in the east. Before 1959 natural disasters on this scale had produced famines in which millions died. In the rural communes the natural shortages were increased by bad local administration. The new government had not enough efficient cadres to run the communes smoothly; to organize the suddenly much complicated working life of the tens of thousands, order the factory and farm raw materials, market, and, above all, estimate production accurately enough for central planning and taxes. Agricultural taxes in China are a percentage of the year's expected harvest. Another percentage, again of the estimated crop, has to be sold to the state at fairly low fixed prices. If the crop is much below the local officials' estimates there will not be enough for the peasants to eat and also for the state quotas.

During the first enthusiasm of the Great Leap Forward, the cadres overestimated the crops and the peasants underproduced. There seems to have been a number of reasons for this underproduction. The one at first most commonly given to the West was that the peasants missed their private gardens and would not work wholeheartedly in the communal fields. What seems, in fact, to have been more important was that the peasants, like everybody else involved in the Great Leap Forward, were muddled and overworked. They wasted time marching about because no one was sure which of the myriad jobs suddenly springing up in the new communes was the most important. They did not know how they were going to be paid: whether on the basis of the hours they worked, what they actually did, the needs of their families, or their political status.

Meanwhile the cadres got the priorities wrong. Work in the fields, and on the more feasible small-scale factory and public-works projects, suffered because they concentrated on producing steel of a uselessly poor quality, bulky goods for which there was no transport, and impressively large scale, but not very useful, dams and canals.

The chaos was cumulative. At the centre, as over-optimistic production figures poured in, the more cautious and realistic local cadres were rebuked or dismissed for the obvious failure their figures showed. The state statistical office, in normal times truthful and sober, could not cope.[39] State investments in heavy industry were made on the basis of inflated promises of agricultural production. Local cadres were unwilling to break local crop failures to the centre, and the centre refused to believe the first reports. Of the 375 million tons of cereal promised for 1959, 125 million tons failed to materialize.

There was, however, no mass starvation or large-scale breakdown of government. Grain, oil, and cotton cloth were strictly rationed; the more expensive foods and most consumer articles were also on a points system of rationing. An individual's ration varied according to the region. He or she was also often asked to set his own eating 'norm'; and it was then a matter of pride and political duty to keep it low. Certain categories of people – housewives, street hawkers, and shopkeepers were expected to eat least. Others – writers, artists, students, and heavy manual workers – had extra rations. In 1960 and 1961 most people were hungry. Few ate fish or meat. The grain ration provided less than the minimum calories needed to maintain normal health. Malnutrition diseases were said to be widespread, particularly in the south. There was some black-marketing and profiteering, and a considerable increase in crime in the big cities; but on the whole rationing worked.

It was not, however, liked. Peasants were increasingly reluctant to give up their grain. There was discontent, and rumours of mutiny in the army. The soldiers, while relatively well fed themselves, had news of bad conditions in their home villages. The number of refugees trying to enter Hongkong increased. Consequently there were unfavourable reports about China in the world press. Even the top communist leadership was not united about the wisdom of the Great Leap Forward policies. And, probably most serious of all, there was an open revolt in Honan in 1961 when militia officers and junior officials turned bandit.

Under these pressures industrial targets were drastically revised. Hundreds of small projects in inaccessible areas were shut down. No more was heard of the backyard steel furnaces, and in the towns most of the urban communes were allowed to wither, and transmute into ordinary cheap restaurants and factories. Most of the street hawkers and small artisans ceased to work within any sort of collec‑tive framework. The towns emptied dramatically. It was said, in 1962 that one million had already left Peking, and another two million were due to go back to the country.

In the villages much of the commune organization broke up. What remained varied from place to place. A general pattern was for most of the commune's functions to be passed to the dozen or more brigades that were its constituent units. The brigades were generally the same size as the old co‑operatives, roughly one large village or several small ones. The brigade is made up of several teams of a few families each, and either the brigade or the team allots work to the families. Again, either the brigade or the team, can be responsible for the general farm plans, marketing, and for the division of the group's profits and the payment of tax and state quotas. The original commune often retains some sort of authority over the brigades, and may be responsible for remaining public works and factories, schools, hospitals, general welfare services, and perhaps the buying of large equipment or another investment of small surpluses. But the commune was discouraged from trying to take more than a small percentage for investment. The major profits were to be distributed by the teams to individuals.

The payment of team members was to be entirely for work done, not according to political reliability. Military commands and drills were not to be used in field work. There were to be no standard issues of necessities. Much of the communal set-up of dining rooms, mending rooms, and nurseries was dissolved, or kept only for rush periods like harvesting. The cadres were told to concentrate on field work, rather than extraneous projects, and not to encourage the peasants to overwork. They were also instructed to avoid rash agricultural schemes, and too much experiment. Within the teams the older peasants were to be consulted, and have their advice taken seriously. 'The Wise Old Peasant', restraining the hotheaded youngsters, or the over-ambitious bureaucrats, suddenly became the popular hero of Chinese plays and newspaper articles. Finally, against the wishes of many cadres, something under ten per cent of the land was returned to individual ownership, and peasants were again encouraged to cultivate their own gardens, and keep their own animals. They were allowed to sell what they had grown in local markets.

The new economic policy was officially defined as investment in agriculture, then light industry, and, last, heavy industry. The central government asked for less grain from the villages. Less machinery was imported, and the growth of heavy industry stopped. Output figures and targets for steel and coal declined for the first time in a decade. What national investment there was in industry in 1961 and 1962 was largely in factories producing goods needed by the peasants – fertilizers and agricultural implements.

There were Western observers who doubted, some with more than a touch of pleasurable anticipation, whether the Chinese economy could recover from the Great Leap Forward. Mr Joseph Alsop in particular received widespread publicity in the United States, and even in Britain, for his theory of 'the declining spiral' in which the Chinese economy was involved.

Fortunately these prophets of famines and disaster were wrong. The 1962 harvest was good, and that year there was an increase in consumer goods and some rations. By 1964 the economic slogan was still 'readjustment, consolidation, filling out, raising standards', and there was still continued emphasis on the need for plain living, hard work and sacrifice. But the shops were full again, most of the queues had gone, and the rice ration had doubled. Fish and fruit were no longer rationed, and were cheap and plentiful. There was more meat and cooking oil.

The Chinese leaders acknowledge that there had been mistakes during the Great Leap Forward. But they deny that the commune movement has been a failure. The economy, they say, is on a sounder basis than it had been in 1957; and the figures support this.

In his *Report on the Work of the Government* given to the Third National People's Congress in December 1964 Chou En-lai claimed that 1962, 1963 and 1964 had all been years of economic recovery and steadily increasing production. 'In 1964', Chou said, 'the total value of industrial output is expected to increase more than 15 per cent over 1963 and to be far higher than in 1957.'[40]

Prices, the Chinese leaders claimed elsewhere, had gone down, and foreign trade up in the mid-sixties. Even the backyard steel furnaces had not been a total loss. They had provided valuable technical training for thousands.

In the country there are solid benefits from the communes. The Chinese villages have more schools, clinics, hospitals, and old people's homes, than any other country in Asia. Many small factories are left, still running, to use local products and provide useful, alternative employment. Above all some of the public works, created at great cost during the heyday of the communes, are on such a scale and of so much agricultural use, as to make a repetition of the disasters of 1959 and 1960 unlikely.

In 1960 the amount of irrigated land was double the 1949 figure. The San Men dam, with the world's third largest reservoir behind it, was finished just too late in 1960 to help the northern drought that year. It will now provide irrigation and prevent drought on 6,600,000 acres. With the San Men and other dams planned for the sixties, or already built on the Yellow River, China's electrical power output will be four times her pre-war figure.

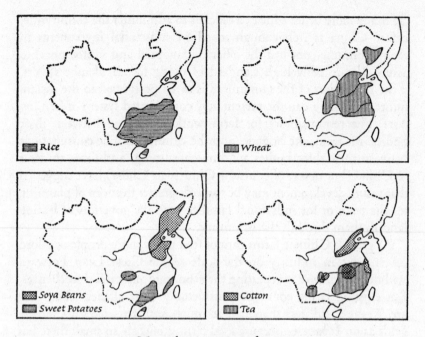

Maps showing principal crops

Nor do the leaders want to discredit the theory of the communes. In 1961 and 1962 cadres were warned to consult the experts, and not to try to make engineering and agricultural decisions on the basis of political theory only. But a few months later correct theory was again all-important. In Kwangtung villagers were told to keep the former rich peasants under constant surveillance. There were official fulminations against the rise of capitalism and hoarding in the countryside. (It was notable that the large increases in food were of vegetables, fruit, pork, eggs and chicken: the products of the peasants' private plots rather than the communally grown cereal crops.)

Chinese leaders have said that the whole commune system will be restored sometime in the future. It must be. It is an essential part of the Chinese government's official reason for existing – the coming of communism. But how soon in the future? Will the leaders be rash enough to try restoring the full communes before there

163

are many more better educated officials to administer the countryside, before China is rich enough to afford substantial investments in each commune (not just the officially favoured and visited ones) to assure a reasonably high standard of living for all members? Yet, if the restoration of the communes is to be postponed to the distant future, how long can the present very complicated system of farming last? The responsibility for farm work is divided between three bodies: the team, the brigade, and the commune. The consultations between these three bodies are time consuming, and some students of China (but never, of course, a Chinese in China) have suggested that future development may be towards greater freedom of planning for the team or for individual families with the government leasing land to them through the commune.

At present Chinese farms cannot feed many more people or afford investments in industry on the scale of the Great Leap Forward without the danger of repeating the economic and civil disturbances. But existing farms could be considerably more efficient than they are. There is still less than half as much fertilizer used on Chinese fields as on Japanese. Because total farm profits are so small there has been little experiment with new methods of rearing stock or new crops. There is not much mechanization. Part of the plan for the communes was that they should be large enough to have their own machinery. But farmers in capitalist countries have co-operative schemes for buying and running machinery. Yet mechanization is unlikely to be successful without education and campaigns for the proper maintenance of machinery. Visitors to Chinese communes have commented on the pieces of machinery left out to rust, and the number of tractors out of order for lack of proper care. Possibly the small rural factories maintained by the communes may teach the elementary rules for the care of machines to a village society which has never had anything to do with them before.

Slightly less than 12 per cent of China is now used for crops. Some of the land is hopeless – desert, mountain, or swamp. But there is land which can be developed, particularly on the western and northern limits of the country. In Sinkiang, around Urumchi, farms run by ex-soldiers on military lines, are very fertile once the

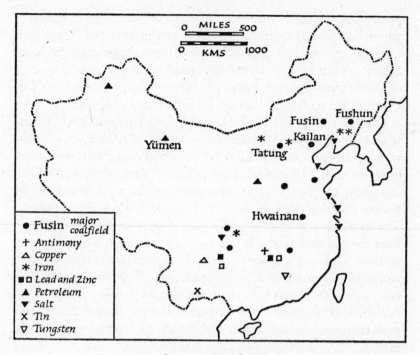

Map showing mineral resources

land is irrigated; and in this new country the fields can be laid out on a large enough scale to make mechanization easy.

Industrially China has adequate but not generous amounts of most metals, coal, and oil (except for aviation fuel). She still needs to import machinery and some manufactured goods. The biggest shortage in China is of good workmen and engineers with modern skills. But among recent testimonies to what the Chinese can achieve are both the atomic bomb and the aircraft instrument landing systems installed in time for the Pakistani airlines to use it.

If China is to survive, both industry and agriculture will have to expand rapidly. This is necessary not only to raise the peoples' living standards to a point at which the communist utopia will have a chance of success; but also just to keep alive a population rapidly increasing beyond the limits of the number who can be fed by

165

present agricultural methods. Recent estimates give China a population of 650 million, increasing at about $2\frac{1}{2}$ per cent a year. Modern medicine, introduced by the communist government, saves babies and adults who would have died in the past; and few, even of China's enemies, can hope that her population problem will be solved in the traditional manner by famine and civil war.

The Chinese at first denied that they had a population problem. It was impossible to have too many people, they said, in a society with a planned economy. Outspoken Peking economists were made to recant their Malthusian errors publicly. Then there was a short campaign to popularize contraceptives. (The explicitness of the posters showing how to use them shocked the foreign visitors.) The campaign, it was said, was to protect women's health, not to limit the population. But it was not very successful. Rubber contraceptives were too expensive, and the cotton waste, the Chinese authorities recommended, was not effective. The new birth control campaign of the sixties has been accompanied by the most outspoken explanations yet given of the dangers of overpopulation. But still the most common argument used is the waste of parental time and the maternal ill-health caused by large families.

Apart from contraception there are propaganda attempts to limit the population. 'Love between men and women', said one of the save-time slogans in 1963, 'is a psycho-somatic activity which consumes energy and wastes time.' Norms are now set for family size. They vary from place to place. Soldiers' wives are generally allowed four children, officials' wives only two. Mothers who exceed their norms are not automatically given maternity benefits or ration books for the new baby. This family limitation is accompanied by moral stories of the prosperity brought by late marriage, and the ruin of good students who married young. In the autumn of 1964 a young toolmaker received nation-wide publicity when he postponed his marriage for the third time to take the opportunity of more technical training offered him. His fiancée, a medical student, wrote that 'she too wished to devote all her energies to her work, and that postponing the wedding would be good for themselves and for the state'.

The right age for a woman to marry is said to be between 23 and 25, and 25 to 29 for a man. (Much later than has been customary in China.) A woman, it is recommended, could have her first baby three or four years after her marriage, but she would be well advised to wait five to eight years for the next. For the father of an overlarge family, sterilization is suggested. Abortion, however, is not encouraged except on medical grounds.

How far these methods of limiting the population will succeed is a key question for China. Most of the developing countries have found it as difficult as Europe did during the Industrial Revolution to make any method of curbing population growth work. But China has means of appealing to her people of a proved effectiveness, and which no other country has or has had.

74 A less than usually fierce expression of China's anti-Americanism. This cartoon of 1963 mocks President Kennedy's 'Strategy for Peace'.

75 Mao Tse-tung, chairman of the Central Committee of the Chinese Communist Party and founder of the Chinese People's Republic, figures in all aspects of culture even the traditional scissor cut.

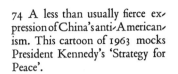

76 Contemporary painters like Fu Pao-shih do not always have to represent political subjects in their pictures. This landscape at Nanking was painted in 1953.

77 (*Below left*) Contemporary literature, particularly poetry, although written in classic style usually pays allegiance to the party. These peasants are having poetry read to them in their lunch-hour.

78 (*Above*) Every New Year paintings with a distinctively communist flavour are hung in public places; this one is to demonstrate the fervour of urban people for the support of agricultural production.

79 (*Right*) These reservoir builders at Miyun are entertained by acrobats.

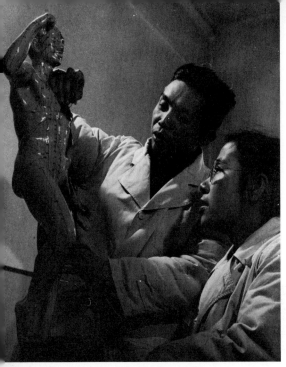

80 (*Left*) Traditional medicine such as acupuncture is still practised in China. A student is taught the various points of the body in which to insert the needle.

81 There have been great advances in Western medicine. This is a medical technician at Shanghai.

82 (*Right*) The Chinese traditional theatre is still performed and respected as an important part of China's culture.

83 The modern theatre performs propaganda plays and operas. This is the first act from the *East is Red* which tells the story of communist victory over capitalism and Nationalist government.

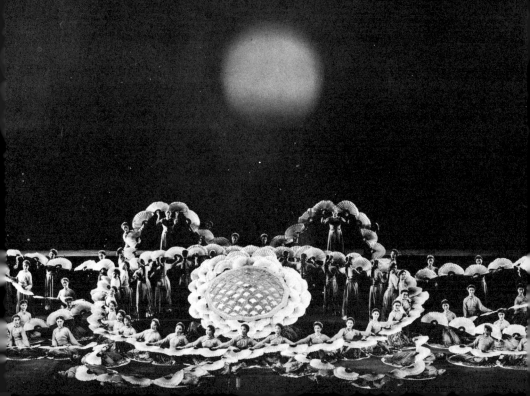

84 Because both their parents are full-time cadres these children board at their nursery, and go home on alternate weekends.

85 The poverty of South China in particular forced the emigration of Chinese to other Asian countries. Some of them made strictly capitalist fortunes, but still want their children educated in China. This school is for Overseas Chinese Children.

86 One of the aims of the 'Great Leap Forward' in 1958 was the raising of the peasant's educational standards. These peasants are being taught to read and write.

87 These working housewives of Peking are being taught the alphabet.

88 When the people are not attending lectures or public meetings in their spare time a visit to the cinema involves further propaganda indoctrination.

89 (*Above*) Outwardly the streets have not changed since pre-communist days. This is at Canton.

90 (*Left*) A shopping arcade at Peking.

10   The New Evangelists

IN 1949 MAO TSE-TUNG MADE HIS FIRST JOURNEY outside
China to arrange Soviet aid for the country he now led. When they
became ministers of newly communist China, Chou En-lai, Chu
Teh, and Liu Shao-chi had last travelled abroad when they went
to Europe as students in the 1920s. After 15 years in Yenan, isolated
in the interior of China, the communist leaders were ignorant of and
prejudiced about the world outside their borders.

From Yenan there had been a possible air and caravan route to the
Soviet Union through the Mongolian desert; but it was little used.
Until a few months before they entered Peking, Stalin continued to
look on the Chinese communists as heretical adventurers without
much hope of success with whom he wanted as little to do as possible.
Few foreigners of any nationality had been to Yenan. (There was an
American military observer group there in the last years of the war,
but no diplomatic corps.) It was physically difficult to get there
through the Japanese or the Kuomintang lines; and those who did
make the journey were often well-wishers with no desire to contradict
any part of the Chinese communist vision.

The less committed journalists, like Edgar Snow,[41] noted the
carefully cultivated foreign sympathies of the Chinese communists
and their irrelevance to what was happening in China. The atrocities and the heroism of the Spanish civil war were debated with
rather more heat than the good and bad of the Chinese civil war.
Franco was utterly condemned, but Mao, at the time of Edgar
Snow's visit, was arranging a United Front with Chiang. There was
an air of unreality in the completeness with which the Yenan communists condemned what they saw as evil foreigners; and the Chinese

virtues with which good foreigners were endowed.[42] Only Chou En-lai, among the top leadership, had had some practical experience of the mixed and un-Chinese qualities of other peoples. He was the communist plenipotentiary who negotiated with the diplomats of Chiang's wartime capital of Chungking. Chou spoke good French and some English. Liu, it is said, spoke Russian. But Mao knew no foreign language.

The communists, including Mao, were, however, well read in Chinese history and literature; far better educated in terms of their own culture than their contemporaries in the Soviet Union, and indeed in much of the rest of Europe. They knew the traditional Chinese picture of China as the centre, or the good governess of the world; the flowery kingdom at whose borders barbarism began. Classically this kingdom was benevolent. Insolence, insubordination and wrong conduct must be rebuked. But barbarians could be civilized by instruction in Chinese custom and by Chinese example.

The Empire's ill-defined boundaries included the now rebellious states of Tibet and Mongolia. Tribute was traditionally due from most of the small, neighbouring countries of South Asia. Tributaries, ambassadors and their trains of merchants might also be received from farther afield. Once they had acknowledged Chinese supremacy, the barbarians ought to be treated with the utmost courtesy and generosity: loaded with gifts and hospitality and sent back to their own uncivilized countries to tell the tale of Chinese superiority. Naturally, however, it was China's duty to decide which of the outer barbarians merited Chinese notice and approval, and which ought to be snubbed or openly rebuked. Great Britain might recognize the Chinese government within days of the communists coming to power. But the long drawn out and humiliating refusal of the Chinese to exchange diplomatic missions[43] would have caused less surprise in London if the Foreign Office had consulted the records of Ch'ien Lung's eighteenth-century dealings with Lord Macartney.

In Yenan, according to Edgar Snow, Mao read every night until the early hours of the morning. His books were partly the Chinese classics and partly the new classics of Marxism. There was little contradiction between them about the world outside China. Marxist orthodoxy reinforced the rigid division into good and evil. It was more than ever China's duty to admonish, and spread the truth. It was even true that many of China's friends and enemies were the same whether they were seen through the leaders' national or through their communist spectacles. The United States particularly had opposed the Chinese communist rise to power; and the Americans were then anxious that Chinese influence should be confined as narrowly as possible.

The major contradiction, perhaps the only contradiction, between the classic and the Marxist Chinese view of their place in the world, was the Soviet Union's claim to be the world's senior Communist Party. To begin with the Chinese did not dispute it. Mao confirmed that the new China would 'lean to one side', the Russian side of world politics. Soviet advice and aid were sought, and Soviet examples quoted.

Reliance on the Soviet Union can never have been an easy policy for the Chinese. From the beginnings of the alliance there were small personal strains. The Russian technicians were highly paid by Chinese standards, and spent freely. The Chinese nickname for them was 'ricebuckets'. Russian drunkenness and their boisterous advances to their girl interpreters were deplorable in the eyes of the puritan communist Chinese. They were similar strains to those between the English and the American servicemen during the Second World War; and as with Britain and America this added up, not to a breach of the alliance, but to the sort of surface irritation which could reinforce less friendly policies if conditions changed.

The Korean War was more serious. It is possible that Stalin encouraged North Korea to invade the south without first consulting China, and perhaps with a view to weakening China's position in Asia. If so, this policy was not entirely successful. Economically China was weakened. Her debt to the Soviet Union and her dependence on Soviet trade was increased by the war; and her industrialization was set back. She was never officially a belligerent. But semi-official 'volunteers' from the Chinese army fought well in Korea. Their courage and their technical skill finally defeated the old picture of the cowardly comic Chinaman current a few years before. After the Korean War the Chinese army was recognized as a most important factor in the East Asian balance of power, with out-of-date equipment perhaps, but with high morale and a well trained officer corps.[44]

In Korea China's principal adversary was the United States: the war confirmed both countries' paranoia about each other. Partly because of Korea the Americans committed themselves with increasing firmness to the policy of the cold war in Asia, anti-communist bastions, and also to the support of Chiang Kai-shek in Taiwan. Military and general aid was poured into the island, and the American fleet patrolled the straits between Taiwan and the mainland. At the height of the cold war it was foolhardy for an American, or a European or Asian in American employ, to question even the standards of Kuomintang government in Taiwan, far less the whole question of whether that government should be there or not. Mainland China, in American eyes, became the Antichrist nation. It was morally impossible that evil, in its Chinese guise, could be recognized by the United States or seated in the United Nations. As late as 1954 Mr Dulles, during the Geneva negotiations that ended the Franco-Vietnamese war, pointedly refused to touch Chou En-lai's outstretched hand.

Mr Dulles was supported by a vocal section of American public opinion, some of it convinced by the views of the late Senator Macarthy, and some of it lulled by the extensive advertising and semi-advertising in the United States on behalf of Chiang Kai-shek and Taiwan. The picture drawn by this advertising of mainland China was of a very weak and a very menacing country. There were American soldiers, politicians, and journalists who alleged both that only an immediate nuclear attack on the relatively defenceless mainland could save the world from total war, and also that the Chinese people were opposed to their government, ripe for rebellion, and would welcome back Chiang's forces. Many Americans (scholars concerned with far eastern affairs and State Department officials) who knew better were restrained by their fear, not only of American public opinion, but also of Asian public opinion. If the United

States abandoned Chiang, so the argument went, her friends in Asia would cease to trust her, and there would be no further confidence in American promises to stem communism. (A similar argument is now used by many Americans in defence of their country's Vietnamese policy.)

Meanwhile the solid Chinese reasons for their enmity with America were similarly increased by the same moral fervour.[45] America had interfered in Chinese affairs. Taiwan was a province of China; only American power sustained it in rebellion. The American fleet, and the American bases in Japan, Okinawa, Taiwan and the Philippines encircled China and menaced her. American intrigues stopped China taking her rightful place as the leader of Asia.

America, in Chinese eyes, was the enemy of all the people in all nations, the supporter everywhere of counter-revolution and foreign domination. She was also 'a paper tiger'. She might seem strong; but if she was firmly resisted she would crumble. Much of the later world anxiety about Chinese aggressiveness and seeming willingness to risk nuclear war goes back to Mao's attempts to reassure his people that America need not necessarily conquer China because she had the more terrible weapons. In support of the same view, Peking Radio broadcast after the Chinese had their own first nuclear explosion, 'The atom bomb is a paper tiger. It is people who decide the outcome of a war, not any weapon.'

Internally, just as it is a common American article of faith that the Chinese hate their government, so it is a Chinese belief that the American people are really China's friends, and only wait for the day when they will be finally delivered from their oppressive bourgeois government. Chinese cartoons show the American worker, dungaree clad, seizing the machine gun from a thin, cowardly, top-hatted Uncle Sam, and leaning over him to shake hands with his beaming Chinese opposite number.[46] Neither the Chinese picture of America nor the American of China is in much danger of contradiction. No Chinese Embassy exists in America. No delegations visit there. Few American reporters are allowed to work in China.

China's view of other countries than America moved closer to reality after the Korean War. China now saw the world as more complicated than it had seemed from Yenan. Not all capitalist countries were equally committed to the cold war. At first Britain was China's favourite European capitalist country. British delegations were received in China, and politely told that China had much to learn from Britain.[47] Later France, after the end of the Vietnamese and Algerian wars, became China's example of a tolerable capitalist country. Franco-Chinese trade increased. Delicate compliments are paid to General de Gaulle.

Even more important was China's discovery of the neutral nations. Like the contemporary United States the Chinese were slow to believe that neutrality could exist. For some years the Chinese rejected Indian advances as coming from a country of British stooges. A peaceful, but genuine, dissolution of empire was impossible. It is said that the behaviour of India as chairman of the Korean Neutral Nations Commission finally convinced the Chinese that the Indians were independent.

The culmination of China's new policy of friendship towards India and her Asian neighbours was the Bandung Conference of 1955, with Chou En-lai beaming at the representatives of nearly every Asian and independent African nation. China's parade of equality with the smallest and brashest of the new nations may not have been altogether convincing. But the newly reasonable China was prepared to negotiate with any of her neighbours about any problems. Burma and China agreed on a settled frontier. Overseas Chinese in most of Southeast Asia were exhorted to learn the language of the country they lived in, send their children to its schools, and take its citizenship. (There continued, however, to be special facilities for Overseas Chinese who wanted to be educated or to retire to the mainland.) With India China negotiated the five principles of co-existence. Chou and Nehru were photographed smiling and clasping each others' hands. Chinese and Indian friendship was to endure a thousand years.

It was not only in Asia that China was freshly seen as a moderate, friendly nation. As the East European states struggled for growing independence after Stalin's death, China intervened against rigid Soviet control; and in particular Chou En-lai's influence was exerted against a Russian military conquest of Gomulka's Poland.

There are Chinese who say now that it was not China who changed after Bandung but the rest of the world who fell out of step with her.[48] Poland was legitimately independent. But Hungary, in China's eyes, was in danger of counter-revolution; and so, rightly re-occupied by Russian forces. Suez, co-incidental with Hungary, sharply reminded China of her old view of treacherous imperialism.

Meanwhile, at home in China, the Hundred Flowers Movement had bloomed, and sharp criticisms of the communists had mounted. This, in the Chinese leaders' eyes, was a warning against lack of zeal in any sphere. As the Hundred Flowers were weeded, and the critics suppressed, Chinese energies were harnessed to the Great Leap Forward. In the dispute about the Great Leap economic policies, moderation led by Chou En-lai was defeated by Liu Shao-chi's zeal and energy.[49] Was there equally a dispute and a victory for zeal over moderation in foreign policies early in 1958?

In the autumn of 1958 the world picture of moderate China was rudely shattered by the Taiwan crisis. Matsu and Quemoy, the islands between Taiwan and the mainland, were shelled, invasion armies were massed on the southeast coast, and communist de-nunciation of the Nationalists mounted. So did promises for Taiwan's protection by the United States and counter threats of invasion of the mainland.

As the shelling and threats to Taiwan gradually diminished, Nehru's India emerged as a sideways victor of the crisis. The West, particularly Britain, had for a long time pointed to India as the alternative model for Asia. In India parliamentary democracy worked, more or less. The state was stable, in marked contrast to other new Asian countries; and the economy, although weak, had suffered no major crisis. The British-trained Indian Army was commonly held to be the best in Asia. India's international prestige benefited, almost equally with China's, from the Bandung Confer-ence. After the Taiwan crisis increasing numbers of Asians saw India as the continent's new strong leader, whose gradual socialism and moderate reforms were better models for Asian revolution than Chinese violence and the exertions of her Great Leap policy.

It was galling for China. It threatened her view of herself both as the historical head of Asia, and as the new model whose revolution was the pattern for all under-developed states in Asia, as in Latin America, and in Africa. There were also solid reasons of national interest to impede the Bandung friendship of Nehru and Chou. While China was weak the British in India had seen Tibet as a usefully independent buffer state. India had accepted the Chinese annexation of Tibet as the re-establishment of Chinese power over a province historically part of the Chinese Empire. But the Western indignation over this conquest found some echoes in India. Tibetan refugees poured into Kalimpong, and Tibetan rebels bought supplies, more or less clandestinely, in India. By 1959 provinces of Tibet were in open revolt, their suppression by the Chinese was bloodthirsty, and the Dalai Lama, the godhead of the Tibetan state, fled with his court to India. Indian sympathies with Tibet mounted. Chinese indignation over the Indian reception of their rebel subjects also mounted.

The Chinese were now firmly established on the borders of India. But the actual frontier with India was still remote from Delhi. It ran through desolate country following the Macmahon line, fixed as an administrative convenience by British civil servants, but never officially agreed to by the Chinese state. Where China did not border India directly, her new neighbours were, to the east, the small, semi-independent Himalayan states: Nepal, Sikkim, Bhutan, and to the west, Pakistan and the state of Kashmir, claimed by both India and Pakistan.

Historically tribute had come to Peking from the Himalayan states. But more recently British India had controlled all their foreign policies. The new India was weaker. Chinese embassies visited the Himalayan states, aid was promised, and treaties of alliance concluded. The first was with Nepal in 1956, although most of the Chinese aid promised then did not materialize.

Meanwhile over the Aksai Chin plateau, in the far north of Indian-controlled Kashmir, the Chinese had built a road linking

Sinkiang and Tibet and running over the Macmahon line into Indian territory. The plateau was so inaccessible from the Indian side that Indian army patrols did not discover the road until several months after its completion. There were then Indian protests, and Chinese claims not only for the Aksai Chin plateau, but also for hundreds of square miles of Indian territory in the Northeast Frontier Province. In the autumn of 1961 the Chinese army broke through the eastern sector of their boundary with India and swept down over the Himalayas to within easy striking distance of the rich plain and cities of Bengal. The Indian army was apparently routed. But the Chinese stopped suddenly, and retreated back almost to their old posts.

There is still speculation about why the Chinese turned back when they did. Its defenders point out that the Indian army had been fighting uphill, and unprepared against the Chinese. Their equipment and their fighting habits were better suited to the plains. There were promises of support for India, possibly nuclear support, from Britain and America. The Chinese may have been misled by Indian Communist Party promises of a rising in Calcutta to coincide with their invasion.

The Chinese had anyway done what they wanted to do. The prestige of the Indian army was shattered. The Indian economy was severely shaken, not only by the losses in the actual fighting (where much equipment had been captured by the Chinese) but also by the consequent popular demand in India that their government should now devote more of its resources to defence. India's position as a rival leader in Asia was further damaged by the new reliance on the West, forced on her by her need for modern armaments. In conferences of neutral nations, Afro-Asian meetings, there was no longer a non-communist great power whose leadership was uncontestable, and whose position privileged her to rebuke and exhort China. India also now 'leant to one side'.

China's first ally, the Soviet Union, had, however, given her little active aid or even diplomatic support over either the Taiwan crisis or the invasion of India.[50] The causes of the growing split between the two communist countries are differently emphasized by every writer on the subject. Some of them at least are personal. After Stalin's death Mao Tse-tung saw himself as the elder statesman of the communist movement: the doctrinal heir of Marx and Lenin. Far from acknowledging his leadership or seeking his advice the new Russian leaders, small men and newcomers in Chinese eyes, denounced Stalin, and so much of the communist past, without even informing the Chinese beforehand.

However, just after Stalin's death the alliance to the outsider had never seemed stronger. Krushchev visited Peking. More credits, more Soviet plans, and Soviet technicians were promised to staff a large number of Chinese enterprises. Three-quarters of China's trade was with the Soviet Union or with other communist countries in the block. There were immense rejoicings in China over the Russian sputnik, and the apparent victory of Russia over the United States in the space race. 'The East wind', said Mao, 'prevails over the West.'

What Mao apparently meant was that now world communism could triumph. Every effort should go into fostering revolution in every country in the world. The final defeat of the United States, imperialism, and capitalism, was at hand. In China itself the Great Leap Forward was to achieve communism in one generation.

In the Soviet Union Krushchev and his advisers had changed the state's economic policy to an increased production of consumer goods. Soviet living-standards went up. The whole country wanted butter not guns, to relax, to live in peace. The Great Leap Forward, the smug Chinese claims, were not only profoundly irritating, but also threatened the Russian position as the world leader of the communist block, and so indirectly her guarantee of the peace of the world.

In 1960 when the Chinese were in the throes of the economic crisis after the Great Leap Forward, the Russians asked for the repayment of all their credits to China, and withdrew their technicians. When the Soviet technicians went they had instructions to take the blueprints for half-built factories and dams with them. One of the reasons given for the withdrawal of the technicians was that the

Chinese were trying to indoctrinate them by making them read Mao Tse-tung.

It was a body blow from which Chinese industry is only just recovering. But for three years, until July 1963, the Chinese and Russians kept an official skin of friendship stretched over the growing breach. The only overt signs of trouble were the clashes on the Sinkiang joint frontier in 1962, and the Chinese reminder to the Soviet Union that the nineteenth-century treaties by which Russia had acquired Chinese-claimed Asian territory were 'unequal'. (The term used for the treaties with the imperialist powers which had been abrogated.) But there were still state references to China and Russia's 'eternal friendship and alliance'. In the months that followed, as the situation deteriorated, China attacked 'right-wing revisionism' in the Russians, but under the thin disguise of attacking Yugoslavia. Similarly the Russians attacked 'left-wing revisionism' in the Albanians, but meant the Chinese.[51]

The Chinese called for no further support for bourgeois nationalists or negotiations with the West. The Russians quoted the Western retreat at Suez as an example of successful pressure on the West. The Chinese quoted Cuba, and the withdrawal of the Russian missiles there, as an example of unsuccessful Russian negotiation.

Several of the world communist countries and parties tried without success to mediate, or at least to preserve their own neutrality. Many of them benefited from the quarrel. Rumania used the breach to further her economic independence. In Asia rival subsidies poured into North Vietnam, North Korea, and Mongolia. Mongolia, hemmed in by the two states, eventually opted for Russia, but continued to receive Chinese aid. North Vietnam has been driven closer to the Soviet Union by the pressure of the war. She continues, however, to receive Soviet arms and Soviet diplomatic support. Over most of the world the greater economic resources and the peaceableness of the Soviet side won over opposition or governing communist parties. But China continued to have considerable internal support in these parties. The Russians angrily accused her of 'splittism'.

By the end of 1963 Russia and China were reviling each other openly. They published long lists of their grievances; and in 1964 there were official Chinese calls for Krushchev's 'liquidation'. For a few months after Krushchev's fall there was a lull in the vilification campaign. The Russian tone continued moderate, but by May 1965 the Chinese were likening Brezhnev to 'that clown Krushchev'. A month later the Soviet leaders were jointly accused of 'practising a more covert, more cunning, and more dangerous revisionism' than Krushchev's.

An important part of the quarrel with the Soviet Union has been over the future of the under-developed world in Africa, Asia, and South America. The Russians are anxious to avoid conflict with the West over these countries. They are also doctrinally convinced that before most of peasant Asian and African countries can become socialist they must have bourgeois and capitalist revolutions. The whole process will take time. For the Russians the new, under-developed nations were of marginal interest before the Chinese forced the competition for their friendship.

To the Chinese immediate revolution ought to be possible in the ex-colonial countries, particularly in Africa, if they know about and follow the Chinese model. China, the message went, was an under-developed country, and had achieved revolution. So could other under-developed countries if they did what China had done. To achieve this end in Africa Sino-African cultural societies are set up throughout the continent. Delegates are invited to Peking, and to tour China. Magazines are distributed, long hours of broadcasting undertaken in the local languages.

The Chinese believe this is essentially educational work, and that it is a sign of contempt to try to sugar the educational pill. The African audience are told about the detailed working of the Chinese revolution. A typical broadcast contains an unshortened leading article from the Peking *People's Daily*, a speech given by the local chairman of the Sino-friendship society, an account of the setting up of a new commune in Inner Mongolia, and the methods used by the third tool factory in Harbin to increase production and cut machine maintenance. The Russians (and the Americans) sweeten their broadcasting with music, cookery hints, and items of local news. The Chinese do not, and their audience has not been large.

For some years the Chinese believed that revolution would come to Africa through local communist parties. One disagreement with the Russians was about the importance of the national bourgeoisie. The Russians wanted to work with them, the Chinese despised them as imperialist dupes. It has, however, not proved easy for the Chinese to find genuine communists in most African countries.

Algeria, on the edge of the Arab and European worlds, has more developed political ideas than most of Africa. For a time Algerian leaders did quote China as a model for their country, and the young Algerian rebels carried (and sometimes read) the works of Mao Tse-tung. But after Algeria won its independence from France the country's leaders and young people became if anything more conventionally nationalist, and less inclined to flirt with world communism and Chinese-type reforms.

In the Congo the Chinese back the rebels against the established government. Here the difficulty was to disentangle communism and class struggle from tribalism and savagery. Elsewhere small opposition parties all over Africa quickly discovered the free-gift system operated by the various ideologies. It is particularly difficult for the Chinese, without the Russian or the American training in anthropology and African custom, to disentangle those who want a landrover bought to forward the cause of international proletarianism, from those who just want a landrover.

The buying of landrovers, the leasing of office premises, and the training of soldiers and politicians is carried on in Africa by the Chinese embassies. But some promising students are sent back to China, although here again the Chinese have been bad pickers. A good many of those chosen for further education in Peking are young men whose academic qualifications are not high enough to get them a scholarship in the West or even in Moscow, and who are anxious for more education from any source available. They are better lodged and fed than their Chinese contemporaries. Some of them, however, have been scornful of Chinese poverty. They have

also been critical about the college teaching, the attempts to indoctrinate them, and the refusal of Chinese girls to respond to their
advances.[52]

Recently the Chinese, in practice although not in theory, have
moved a little away from their goal of immediate communist
revolution in Africa. In June 1965 Chou En-lai was heavily
snubbed when he announced, during his visit to Tanzania, that
'an exceedingly favourable situation for revolution prevails today
not only in Africa but also in Asia and Latin America'. The Kenyan
government, which a few weeks before had seized Chinese lorries
and arms on their way across its territory, replied, 'the Kenyan
government intends to avert all revolutions irrespective of their
origins...'. Contrary to previous expectations Chou was not invited
to Kenya, Uganda, Zambia, Congo (Brazzaville), or the Central
African Republic. On his return to China his speeches talked of
Africa as 'ripe' only for 'anti-imperialist revolution'.

China was, at the same time, beginning to realize that few
African countries had left-wing oppositions capable of seizing
power. Chinese support for ineffective local communists only drove
the new African governments into world support for Russia or the
West. Increasingly, Chinese friendship is offered to any new country
ready to declare itself hostile to imperialism.[53] Today to qualify for
Chinese aid, a country need not cut its ties with the West or cease to
receive Western aid.

In Tanzania during the reception of Chou En-lai in June 1965
a correspondent noticed that the guard of honour was armed with
Chinese rifles; but the salute accorded Chou was fired from British
25-pounders. The purpose of Chinese aid to countries like Tanzania
is to win unexclusive friendship, and leave the heads of the government thinking, in the words of President Nyerere at the time of the
Commonwealth Peace Mission to Vietnam, 'we believe that the
Chinese are people too'.[54] It is a policy that is likely to become more
successful as China's past reputation for backing impractical hot-
heads fades.

Between 1960 and 1965 China promised about $150 million as
aid to Africa, only a quarter of which was actually disbursed. This is

a considerable sum in terms of Chinese revenue, but much less than Western or even Russian credits to the countries concerned. But China has shown more imagination in the distribution of her aid than she does in her verbal or written propaganda. Earlier China sent 15 tons of grain to Guinea just as her difficulties after her drastic break with France were at their height. Chou En-lai is believed to have offered over £75 million to the governments of Tanzania and Zambia to build a railway linking the Zambia copper belt to the sea, thus freeing Zambia from her present dependence on the transport system of the white Rhodesian government.

The Chinese claimed at a recent meeting of the Afro-Asian People's Solidarity Organization that they were 'coloured, and your blood brothers in the struggle' (against imperialism). They have attempted to exclude the Russians from Afro-Asian meetings, and the Russians retorted that the Chinese are 'backward, poor, chauvinist and racialist'. Nor has the Chinese assertion of fraternity with Africans always rung quite true in countries where the smiles of a touring Chou En-lai or Chu Teh were backed by the grim disapproval of their aides and their rejection of all local friendly advances. Chinese technicians, helping with Chinese financed projects in Africa and Asia have orders to live as the local people do and eat local food. Their puritanism, however, makes less appeal in Africa than in Asia; and orders have recently, it is said, gone out to Chinese embassies in Africa to give more parties of a type that are popular locally.

In Asia, Chinese aid to non-communist, as well as the communist, states has been on a larger scale than her aid to Africa. The Chinese model is particularly applicable to Asian conditions (the Vietcong have been encouraged to fight a guerrilla war closely, and not always appropriately, modelled on the Chinese civil war). Chinese puritanism, Chinese university conditions, and heavy-handed Chinese propaganda are less inappropriate in Asia, where most Asians share some of the Chinese sentiments, than they are in Africa. On the other hand Southeast Asia was traditionally part of the Chinese tributary empire. There is an historic distrust of China added to by fear of the use China might make of the Overseas

Chinese communities. Much of this fear was allayed at Bandung; and, since Bandung, while Chinese policy has hardened in the rest of the world, it has stayed in general conciliatory and friendly to her smaller, south Asian neighbours. There has been no reversal of the Peking policy of gradual disassociation with the south Asian Chinese. It would probably be an even less gradual dissociation if China did not need the money sent her by these communities, and if she was not faced by the nationalists' insistence on Taiwan as an alternative focus for Overseas Chinese loyalties.

Yet, in the 1960s, South Asia was the most explosive region in the world. In its unhappy countries the United States and China fought out what was both their crusade against the other's ideology, and the battle for territories both nations thought essential for their national security. Their allies: western Europe, Britain, and the old dominions behind the United States; the Soviet Union behind China, gave some verbal support and occasional practical aid. Their main concern, however, was to moderate the ardours of their champions short of total war.

China, even more than the United States, hindered rather than helped her cause by the ferocity of her language, and the occasional ineptness of her diplomacy. Yet the Chinese, like the Americans, were eager for any allies in the region including those who did not support either Chinese communism or American capitalism as the guiding light for their countries.[55] Cambodia did particularly well out of aid given her by every power with interests or ambitions in the region.

Of the Asian battlegrounds Indonesia has been one of the bloodiest and least publicized. These rich islands, where the central government never succeeded in controlling the outlying provinces, were the victims of a series of right- and left-wing army coups. In the early 1960s the Indonesian Communist Party was the world's largest outside the countries with communist governments; and its leaders accepted the Chinese, not the Soviet, view of communism. The party's influence was, however, severely damaged by the reprisals during the suppression of Colonel Untung's attempted coup in the autumn of 1965. Over 100,000 communists, suspected communists and locally unpopular villagers were shot, and those Indonesian communist leaders who survived went into hiding. The triumphant generals were pro-Western in their sympathies. Chinese consulates were sacked, Chinese nationals killed, and Chinese policy and advice derided.

Further to the West China's alliance with the military dictatorship of Pakistan was a diplomatic triumph. Pakistan had been one of the allies the West took most for granted, and her new alliance became the showpoint for Chinese spokesmen eager to demonstrate to the world China's ready friendship for any non-imperialist nation whatever the colour of its internal government. The alliance was founded on both countries' enmity to India. The Sino-Indian border dispute was still unsettled; and over Kashmir Pakistan had been able to obtain no solid support for her claims from the West or from the Soviet Union. For China her new friendship had the additional advantage of weakening the Western organized military alliances of which Pakistan was a member.

In the 1965 Indo-Pakistani war over Kashmir the alliance was of more practical value to Pakistan than to China. Chinese threats kept Indian troops away from the Kashmir fighting, and contributed to Indian readiness to negotiate. But China did not occupy the remaining territory she claimed on the Tibet border, probably because she was afraid of provoking a major war if her troops entered India.

The danger of a major Asian war was at its most acute in Vietnam. The Chinese were naturally afraid of the establishment of a possibly hostile state on their vulnerable southwestern border; and they gave verbal and some material aid to the North Vietnamese communists. China and Vietnam, the Chinese said, are bound together as 'the lips and teeth'. On the other side the Americans too could not accept the total loss of Vietnam to their camp. It would, they claimed, damage their prestige throughout the world, and jeopardize those Asian bases which (since Pearl Harbour) many Americans had seen as the front line closely guarding San Francisco.

Chinese statements on the Vietnamese war stressed China's readiness for immediate war with the United States. Southwestern

Chinese cities were prepared for air raids, and the army warned of the likelihood of war . . . and the impossibility of China's defeat in her just cause. But China's actions were less belligerent than her leader's speeches. The North Vietnamese were urged not to nego-tiate; but Chinese 'volunteers' were not sent to fight in Vietnam as they had been sent to Korea. North Vietnam was kept short of weapons China could have supplied. The Chinese airforce in par-ticular could have made a considerable difference to Vietnamese defence against air raids; but neither its planes nor its pilots were used.

In the short term perhaps the best that Southeast Asia can hope for is a more rigid division between the Chinese and the American spheres of influence and so a more limited scope for local wars and coups. The long-term prospects are more hopeful. Given time, some of the region's specific problems will solve themselves. In Taiwan, one of the region's powder kegs, Chiang Kai-shek is an old man. His successors, it is said, have their plans to make peace with Peking ready. Taiwan will be recognized as an autonomous region (like Sinkiang-Uighur or Tibet), controlling its own internal policies, but with its external policies subject to mainland Chinese control. Hints from Peking, from Taiwan itself, and most of all from Hongkong, add supporting details to this story. There is even a ver-sion, hopefully told, which sees Taiwan as continuing to receive American economic aid, although the American Seventh Fleet will no longer be needed for its protection.

If the Chinese really believe that the Americans, in the present state of the world, will be happy to go on contributing large sums of money to a Chinese autonomous region, it is one more example of their dangerous ignorance of other countries. It is the sort of mistaken thinking that increases world danger of war; and it is heavily con-tributed to by the isolation that the West has forced on China.

However, it seems unlikely that United States' diplomacy can continue indefinitely (even if it wishes to do so), to reserve China's seat in the United Nations to the Taiwan government; and when China becomes a member of the UN her representatives will also serve on a number of associated international bodies. Some of the present denigration of the United Nations, and the drawing up of unacceptable terms on which China would be prepared to join the UN, may be due to the Chinese leaders' reluctance to allow their junior diplomats this experience of practical international co-operation. But the Chinese are prepared to allow delegations and students to visit Britain, learn English, and study British institutions. This practical demonstration to both Chinese and Britons that neither side corresponds to the stock caricatures of communism or imperialism could be enlarged by scholarships, inviting more delegations of skilled adults, and by official and unofficial hospitality.

Contact with younger Chinese is of particular value now because there is evidence that (like the Nationalists on Taiwan) the second generation of Chinese communists may be more open to compromise settlements than their elders. And the elders are now very old men. (A part of the present critical situation in Asia has been the natural impatience of the old who want to see the millennium revealed in their own time.) The present Chinese leaders are certainly afraid that their successors will be less ardent in the cause of world revolution than they are themselves. No propaganda theme since 1949 has been as stressed for so long as the lesson on continuing revolution. Communism, the Chinese young are told, may take tens, hundreds of years, but it is their duty to continue to strive for it. They must live all their lives austerely, and resist both the blandishments of the Russian Revisionists, and the tricks of the West. Yet the young at one level still show an inclination for easy living, nylon suits and jazz; and at another for the moderate arguments of the Soviet Union and peace in their time. Are the elders going to win, and the young continue to be pledged to the crusade for world revolution? Or will the next generation follow the path of all previous second generation revolutionaries towards compromise, caution, and the subordination of their elders' dangerous enthusiasms to more soberly considered national interests? No one outside or inside China, seems certain of what the outcome will be and what Mao's successors will be like.

91 The example and leadership of Mao Tse-tung has inspired China's people. Here he is inspecting health work at Hangchow in 1958.

92 The 'Great Leap Forward' of 1958 instigated by Mao forced the pace of industrialization. This coking plant at a rural steel centre established a daily output of 1,000 tons.

93 Sung Ching Ling is the vice-chairman of the People's Republic of China and widow of Sun Yat-sen. 94 Chou En-lai, the Premier of China was one of the founders of the revolution.

95 China claims a People's Army of 120 million strong.

96 An enthusiastic army of peasant workers during a spring afforestation campaign.

97 The Yangtsze bridge is one of the proudest achievements of the present government. China, however, is only partially a modernized nation, and the traditional junk is still the commonest form of water transport.

98 At this commune iron smelting is carried out by primitive methods.

99 (*Above*) Traditional industry continues and is not always replaced with modern methods. This is salt-mining at Tseliutsin.

100 (*Below*) The communists have developed new oil wells. This oil refinery employing modern techniques still uses mule transport.

101 In 1958 the emphasis in the commune was on militarized discipline. At the Weising Commune the peasants obey the bugle call.

102 Everyone must participate in industrial production. Women workers at a factory canteen.

103 During their leisure hours these commune members relax at a rural cultural centre.

104 (*Left*) A poster in Peking urges the liberation of Taiwan the seat of the banished Nationalist government in 1956.

105 In the 1958 hostilities between mainland China and Taiwan (which was supported by the United States), this pilot who had been doing reconnaissance on Chiang Kai-shek's orders was captured and arrested by the communists.

106 (*Right*) Relations between the Soviet Union and China were outwardly friendly in 1957 when Mao Tse-tung and Krushchev met in Moscow. A rift developed between the two countries from the late 1950s over the leadership of world communism.

107 In 1955 at the Bandung Conference China adopted a peaceful and benevolent attitude to India and her Asian neighbours. Her later claims of Indian territory precipitated the war of 1961. The Chinese withdrew after a few months; these Indian prisoners were allowed to observe their religious festivals.

避孕方法介绍

108 An important challenge to China's future is the control of her population. A new move advocating family planning was instigated in 1962 with the publication of a series of posters. This is the first of the series and the caption reads: 'An introduction to the avoidance of pregnancy'.

Notes on the Text

2 COLONIZING CHINA

1   But the title of the first Chinese of all must go to Peking Man, whose bones, the earliest of human type found in China, are about half a million years old.

2   After Ch'in Shih-huang-ti's death legalism became a dirty word in China. Confucianism was the respectable code. Legalist ideas, however, continued to influence later emperors and their advisers. A Legalist ancestry has been claimed, by its enemies, for Chinese communism.

3   See Cottrell, L., *The Tiger of Ch'in*, London, 1962.

4   The military strategy, however, was less to try and stop the barbarians breaking through than to pin them back against the wall once they had broken through. It was a similar theory to that which the Romans had about the use of their British wall against the Picts and Scots.

5   Even in the parts of the country where all tigers have long been exterminated, they are the wild animals of legends, proverbs and fairy stories – like wolves in Western Europe.

6   Wang Chien, *c.* 756–835. Translated A. Waley, *Chinese Poems*, London, 1946.

3 THE ORDER OF SOCIETY

7   An un-Roman administrative tradition: more human but less convenient for the central power.

8   Fried, M. H., *The Fabric of Chinese Society*, London, 1956.

9   Mostly of course, it was an aspiration for the middle aged and settled. The revolt, passive or active, of young Chinese against their large families is the theme of a line of novels from the eighteenth-century *Dream of the Red Chamber* to the modern novelist Pa-chin's *The Family*. In both novels cousin lovers, brought up together, are forced apart by the tyranny of their family elders.

10 J. Lossing Buck, *Land Utilization in China*, Chicago, 1937.

11 Apart from the emperor and the members of his immediate family, the only Chinese given any hereditary respect were the descendants of the philosophers, particularly the Kung family, the descendants of Confucius. But even the Kung family had none of the powers of the aristocracy in Europe.

12 Quoted, Ho Ping-ti, *The Ladder of Success in Imperial China*, Columbia, 1962.

13 Op. cit.

14 Like Chou En-lai's family.

15 The classic view of foreigners was given by Mencius. 'I have heard of men using the doctrines of our great land to change barbarians, but I have never yet heard of any being changed by barbarians.'

16 The Ming was a particularly and consciously conservative dynasty: a national reaction to the foreign Yüan dynasty and its international con-nexions through the other countries conquered by the Mongols. Ming scholars, painters, poets, as well as the government, tried to return, not altogether successfully, to the all-Chinese culture of the Sung and T'ang.

17 We are sometimes said to smell so revolting to the Chinese because we eat butter and cheese and drink milk, which they do not. We also nowadays wash ourselves and our clothes considerably less.

18 The Chinese craftsmen faithfully reproduced the details of dress, even the shockingly low necklines and bare feet of European peasant women and goddesses. (Dresses were, and are, cut high in China; and even when their feet are unbound and the rest of their clothes are rags, Chinese women always wear shoes. Female throats and feet are erotically stimulating in China.) But what the Chinese craftsmen could not bring themselves to believe in were the foreign eyes. Prince Charles Edward, the rose and gold Venus, and the buxom peasants all have narrow, slightly slanting eyes.

19 Quoted D. E. T. Luard, *Britain and China*, London, 1962.

20 Riders carrying official letters, made excellent speed for horsemen, over the post roads. But it was still a matter of weeks from the western frontiers to Peking.

21 Feuerwerker, A., *China's Early Industrialization*, London, 1959.

22 The name given them by foreigners at the time. Their proper Chinese

name is still much disputed. The most generally accepted translation is
'the Fists of Righteous Harmony'.

5 THE COMMUNISTS

23 *Land and Labour in China*, London, 1932. In this most prescient and readable
of economic surveys of China Tawney noted that 'the revolution of 1911
was a bourgeois affair. The revolution of the peasants has still to come. If
their rulers continue to exploit them, or to permit them to be exploited as
remorselessly as hitherto, it is likely to be unpleasant. It will not, perhaps,
be undeserved.'

24 To contemporary Westerners sympathetic to the idea of a strong reformed
China, the communists were a distraction and a nuisance. They did not
appear to outsiders as a serious problem, far less an alternative government.
But, while they existed, they stopped plans for reform by absorbing
Chiang's attention, and using men and money in the expensive civil war.

25 See 'The Long March' by Anthony Garavente in the *China Quarterly*,
No. 22. Mr Garavente argues convincingly that the figures for the army
losses show that the Long March was a communist defeat.

26 See the translations of some of Mao's poems in an appendix to Jerome
Ch'ên's and Michael Bullock's *Mao and the Chinese Revolution*, London,
1965. This is the most recent and authoritative history of the communists
and biography of Mao up to 1949.

27 At the beginning of the Long March there was probably no intention of
taking the Red Army as far as the remote and poverty-stricken province of
Shensi. It was part of Mao's political victory during the March that he
took the major part of the army northwards, instead of trying to establish
a base in the far west.

28 Quoted Pannikar, K. M., *In Two Chinas*, London, 1955.

29 This was to be a pattern repeated several times in Asia, notably in Vietnam, where other foreign armies (French and then American) relied again
on strong-points and the control of the cities. And again were unsuccessful
in holding the country against a hostile peasantry.

7 THE UNIFIED STATE

30 Lifton, J. R., *Thought Reform*, London, 1961. This is a detailed and
interesting study of brain-washing in Chinese prisons and outside by a
professional psychiatrist.

31 Another piece of evidence much quoted some years ago is the behaviour of
the 21,000 Chinese prisoners-of-war in Korea. They were offered the

choice of returning to their homes and families in China, or going to Taiwan. 14,000 chose exile in Taiwan. It has been argued that two-thirds of the Chinese people would similarly welcome the return of the Kuomintang in place of the communists.

It is a shaky argument because it is not clear just what the reasons were which sent the 14,000 to Taiwan. They may have been ex-Kuomintang soldiers from the armies which had surrendered to the communists, and who did not take their new loyalties more seriously than their old. Another, more sinister, explanation was, in part, put forward by the Chinese at the time of the peace negotiations. The prisoners in camps in South Korea had been roughly, and probably inaccurately, grouped according to whether they were communist or non-communist. The majority were grouped as non-communist. The administration of all the camps was very independent of the American guards; and the non-communist camps were partly staffed by Chinese Nationalists. (There were too few Chinese-speaking UN soldiers.)

When an International Commission was sent to interview soldiers from both sides who refused repatriation, the majority of the Chinese never saw the Commission. (Mostly because of UN procedural delays.) Those who did see it are said to have been carefully selected by the Nationalists. The tortured bodies found in the camps (both communist and non-communist) and the 'suicides' were of those unfortunate prisoners who had dissented from the camp's political direction.

8 NEW SCHOLARS AND ARTISTS

32 *Soviet Scientist in China*, London, 1964. Professor Klochko asked for political asylum in Canada in 1961, and his book was first published in New York.

33 Seemingly innocent classical designs are as dangerous to craftsmen as they are to writers or artists. The *Ta-Kung Pao* newspaper reported in October 1964 that the Ceramic Research Centre of the Kantan Pottery Company had a decorative design on some of their products called 'Fishing, Tree-Felling, Tilling the Land and Reading'. The drawing shows 'a scholar reading a book in a pavilion on the upper side of the picture and fishermen, woodcutters and peasants toiling in the foreground'. At a workers' discussion group on the subject, it was claimed that the picture 'sought to promote the reactionary idea of Mencius' that 'the scholastic pursuit is above all other callings', and 'those who do mental labour rule the people and those who do manual labour are ruled by others'.

208

34 George Orwell in *The Prevention of Literature* first noticed that totalitarianism need not be 'so deadly' for poetry as for prose. 'Bureaucrats despise poets', he said, 'and so do not bother about them.' Secondly, what the poet says, 'That is what his poem means if translated into prose – is relatively unimportant . . . a poem is an arrangement of sounds and associations, as a painting is an arrangement of brushmarks . . . it is therefore fairly easy for a poet to keep away from dangerous subjects and avoid uttering heresies.' This is more applicable to the relatively inefficient Russian totalitarianism of the 1930s and 40s than it is to China today; but poetry still remains far livelier and freer in China than prose.

35 There is an interesting collection of papers on modern Chinese literature in the *China Quarterly*, No. 13.

9 BUILDING PERFECTION

36 *Political Quarterly*, July–Sept. 1963.

37 Jan Myrdal in his book *Report from a Chinese Village*, London, 1965, describes the formation of collectives and a commune in the north Shensi village where he worked. In this village clearly the most dramatic and difficult step for the revolutionary peasants was the formation of the first collective.

38 There are two sorts of militia units in China. The roughly trained groups to which all adult young men and many women belong; and the better equipped, more highly trained special militia units for party members and volunteers.

39 The value of Chinese statistics has been much disputed. Most of them always have been in comparative form; and sometimes the comparison has been with pre-war years when production generally, or of the particular item cited, was notably low. Up to 1957 most economists accept the Chinese figures as accurate. Thereafter there is a period of muddle, followed by a great scarcity of any figures at all. More plentiful economic data is now available about the Chinese economy; but some economists are still doubtful about the accuracy of all the figures given.

40 Philip L. Bridgham discussing Chou En-lai's report in the *China Quarterly* (April–June 1965, No. 22) points out that on a *per capita* basis China in 1965 would continue to lag behind 1957 because of the large population increase (eight to one hundred million) in the eight-year interval. Mr Bridgham also has doubts about Chou's claims for cotton and pig production, for the great increase in steel production, and for the 15 per cent rise in total industrial output. He accepts Chou's other claims.

41 His book *Red Star over China* published in 1937, still contains not only one of the most vivid of the pictures of contemporary Yenan, but also a description of the communist aims and methods, and biographies of the leaders which are still of great value.

42 This popular involvement with foreign countries has continued. Travellers testify to their astonishment on finding in remote interior villages posters expressing sympathy with the Algerians, and demonstrations in support of the Dominican left wing. Students in Lanchow and Chungking are eloquent about the Congolese or the Cubans. It is in some ways a major change from imperial China where most Chinese were both ignorant and uncaring about foreigners. But present-day Chinese knowledge sees (and even, on the posters, draws) the foreigners as unfortunate Chinese domiciled in the harsh outside world. Any idea that the foreigners may have different systems of thought is completely missing from the Chinese picture of them.

43 The Chinese still refuse to exchange ambassadors. The British Mission in Peking and the Chinese mission in London are each headed by a Chargé d'Affaires.

44 Probably still a fairly true picture. Apart from their atomic bomb Chinese arms and aeroplanes are old fashioned by the standards of other Asian countries, like India, which have been armed by the West. Chinese soldiers are conscious of themselves as an *élite*, however, and are well-trained and disciplined. Staff work, movement of supplies, intelligence, all appear to be good if somewhat hidebound by the traditions of the good old days of the Long March and Yenan.

45 There is a suggestion that some of the peculiar bitterness of the two countries' relationship is because modern China is, in a way, America's child. For 20 years before 1949 China had been the favourite target of American good works. American missionaries set up schools and hospitals in China; American diplomats, at any rate in theory, protected China against the excesses of the imperialist powers. American students took Chinese past and present civilization seriously when the rest of the world jeered. The Americans could have been sympathetic, helpful, and generous to a Chinese revolution they approved of. They were snubbed.

46 To begin with the Chinese saw much of the world in terms of wicked governments and good people. They believed that they could appeal effectively over the heads of the governments through the various 'peace' organizations. When it became clear that these peace organizations were

not truly popular, the Chinese used them less; and in all major countries, except the United States, strengthened their knowledge and ties of the government and the official hierarchy.

47 Although as late as 1954 when a British Labour Party Delegation toured China, they were firmly told by Chinese officials that the British National Health Service could not exist.

48 This is a Hongkong view. Chinese in Hongkong, whether communists or Nationalists, will make general statements about their leaders' policies with a freedom lacking on the mainland or in Taiwan. They are often well-informed statements; semi-official, inspired at a high level, and very useful to governments whose totalitarian structure makes it difficult for them otherwise to try out opinion; or air internal differences.

49 See Roderick MacFarquhar 'Communist China's Intraparty Dispute', *Pacific Affairs*, December 1958.

50 Over the invasion of India, China later criticized the Soviet Union's failure to support her as 'a betrayal'; and, in his long speech on the quarrel in 1964, M. A. Suslov talked of the 'pernicious consequences' of the Chinese invasion; and the 'grave harm' it inflicted on 'the national liberation movement, the progressive forces of India and the entire front of the anti-imperialist struggle'. But neither side was so outspoken in 1961.

51 'Revisionism', revising or altering the sacred text of Marx, Lenin, and Stalin is a cardinal sin in the communist world. It is difficult for a Westerner to know just how much weight to attach to the doctrinal quarrels of communism. Because the founders of communism were prolific, texts can be found to back most points of view. Non-communists are tempted to the belief that the point of view is arrived at, and the text to back it then searched out. But this is probably an over-cynical view of, at any rate, the Chinese side of the quarrel. (Educated Moslems presumably said much the same about the Christian struggles of the Thirty Years War.)

52 See E. Hevi, *An African Student in China*, London, 1965.

53 This policy received doctrinal backing in June 1963, when in 'A Proposal Concerning the General Line of the International Communist Movement', the Chinese analysed the four 'fundamental contradictions in the contemporary world'. They were between the communist and non-communist worlds, between classes in capitalist countries, between 'oppressed nations' and imperialism, and among imperialist countries. Of these the conflict between the imperialists and the oppressed nations was said to have most importance at present.

54 To mark his friendship with the Chinese people President Nyerere constantly wears the uniform of a Chinese cadre. Or this is what he says. The suits are indeed blue; but open necked and made of silk.

55 Even that bastion of old-fashioned free enterprise, Hongkong, notched into the mainland of South China, has been growled at from Peking. But it continues to be supplied with food and water from the mainland; and its existence (for good reason) is not seriously threatened. Many Chinese trade agreements with the West are arranged through the branch of the Bank of China in Hongkong. Dollar and pound foreign remittances to China from the Overseas Chinese are also sent through this Bank. Visas are commonly issued in Hongkong; and the colony serves as an economic safety valve for the province of Kwangtung. (Most of the Hongkong refugees are fleeing from poverty rather than political persecution.) Communist and Western publications are both freely available to students of either block. Macao has similar uses. The colony is less officially tolerant; but the police are less efficient.

Select Bibliography

Harris, R., *Modern China*, National Book League, London, 1961. This is an excellent introductory bibliography with short notes on the books suggested. Among the books either not mentioned or since published I found the following particularly interesting:

Ch'ên, J., *Mao and the Chinese Revolution*, London, 1965

Cottrell, L., *The Tiger of Ch'in*, London, 1962

Dawson, R. (ed.), *Legacy of China*, London, 1964

Fitzgerald, C. P., *China: A Short Cultural History* (rev. ed.), London, 1950

Fu-Sheng, M., *The Wilting of the 100 Flowers*, London, 1962

Gernet, J., *Daily Life in China on the Eve of the Mongol Invasions*, London, 1962

Greene, F., *The Curtain of Ignorance*, London, 1965

Greene, F., *The Wall Has Two Sides*, London, 1962

Grousset, R., *The Rise and Splendour of the Chinese Empire*, London, 1952

Klochko, M. A., *Soviet Scientist in China*, London, 1964

Lundquist, S., *China in Crisis*, London, 1965

Mehnert, K., *Peking and Moscow*, London, 1963

Myrdal, J., *Report from a Chinese Village*, London, 1965

Needham, J., *Science and Civilization in China*, London, 4 vols., 1954–62

Newman, R. P., *Recognition of Communist China*, New York, 1961

Prodan, M., *Chinese Art*, London, 1958

Roy, C., *Into China*, London, 1955

Snow, E., *The Other Side of the River*, London, 1963

Sullivan, M., *An Introduction to Chinese Art*, London, 1962

Swann, P., *Chinese Painting*, London, 1958

Swann, P., *The Art of China, Korea and Japan*, London, 1963

Waley, A. (trs.), *Chinese Poems*, London, 1961

Watson, W., *China*, London, 1961

Wint, G., *Communist China's Crusade*, London, 1965

Wood, S., *A Street in China*, London, 1958

The China Quarterly is the leading non-communist journal devoted to Chinese affairs.

Among the journals published in Peking and available in Britain, *China Reconstructs* is the liveliest and most easily obtainable.

Acknowledgements

The author wishes to thank Mr Guy Wint for having read this book in manuscript.

Photographs were supplied by the following: from W. Alexander, *Costume of China*, London, 1805, 27; from T. Allom and G. N. Wright, *China Illustrated*, London, 1943, 26; by courtesy of the Ashmolean Museum, Oxford, 4; Associated Press, 42, 46, 47, 48, 59; by courtesy of The British Council for the Promotion of International Trade, 108; by courtesy of the Trustees of the British Museum (Natural History), 3; by courtesy of the Trustees of the British Museum, 5, 6, 9; Camera Press Ltd (China News Service), 7, 8, 13, 14, 17, 18, 20, 40, 41, 49, 60, 61, 62, 64, 65, 66, 67, 68, 69, 70, 71, 72, 73, 74, 75, 77, 78, 79, 80, 86, 87, 88, 89, 90, 91, 92, 93, 94, 95, 96, 98, 101, 102, 105, 106, 107; Cartier Bresson, 53, 54, 55, 56, 57, 58, 82; China Inland Mission, 15, 16, 36, 43, 51; China Missionary Society, 12, 34; from J. B. de Halder *Description de l'Empire de la China*, Paris, 1735, by courtesy of the Trustees of the British Museum, 23, 24, 28; S. Farnell, 97; Imperial War Museum, 38; Lois Mitchison, 19, 63, 81, 84, 85, 100, 104; National Army Museum, Camberley, 31, 39; New China News Agency, 44, 83, 103; by courtesy of the Parker Gallery, London, 32; by courtesy of the Royal Academy of Arts, London, 30; from G. Staunton, *An Authentic Account of the Embassy to the Emperor of China*, London, 1797, by courtesy of the Trustees of the British Museum, 21; 25, Photo the *Sun*, 45, 50, 52; from J. Thomson, *Illustrations of China and its People*, London, 1873, 11, 33; from P. van Hoorn, O. Dapper (ed.), *Gedenkwaerdig Bedryf der Nederlandsche oost Indische Maetschappye op de Kuste en in Lef Keizernijk van Taising von Sino*, Amsterdam, 1670, by courtesy of the Trustees of the British Museum, 22.

Acknowledgement is also made to the following publishers whose books are quoted: George Allen and Unwin Ltd, from A. Waley (trans.), *Chinese Poems*, 1946 on pp. 19, 20; from K. M. Pannikar, *In Two Chinas*, 1955 on p. 84; Chatto and Windus, from D. E. T. Luard, *Britain and China*, 1962 on p. 57; Columbia University Press, from Ho Ping-ti, *The Ladder of Success in Imperial China*, 1962 on p. 35.

Who's Who

CHEN YI, b. 1901. Became Foreign Minister in 1958. His previous reputation was as a military leader against the Japanese and the KMT, and as administrator. He is Chairman of the National Defence Council, and has accompanied Chou En-lai on several foreign tours. He is a keen chess player, interested in football, and writes poetry.

CHEN YUN, b. 1905. China's leading economist, and a member of the Politbureau, a deputy premier, and Deputy Chairman of the CCP (Chinese Communist Party) Central Committee. He criticized the more extreme of the Great Leap Forward policies in March 1959, and suffered some political reverse as a result; but he is now largely reinstated except that he ranks second, not as before first, among the deputy premiers.

CHIANG KAI-SHEK, b. 1887. The President of the Republic of China (Nationalist). The head of the Kuomintang government in Taiwan (Formosa) which claims also to be the rightful government of mainland China. After Sun's death and the Kuomintang split Chiang was the ruler of China from the 1920s to his defeat in 1949.

CH'IEN LUNG (1711–99). The 4th Emperor of the Manchu (Ch'ing) dynasty. Conquered Sinkiang. With China at its zenith of external security and internal prosperity Ch'ien Lung rejected the proposals for alliance and trade made him by George III of England.

CH'IN SHIH-HUANG-TI (259–210 B.C.). Completed Ch'in conquest of Chou feudatory states of North China. By ruthless methods unified a larger empire in China than any of his predecessors. Built the Great Wall, burnt the Confucian books, and killed protesting scholars.

CHOU EN-LAI, b. 1898. Prime Minister, the third man in the CCP hierarchy (after Mao and Liu), and until 1958 Foreign Minister. Chou has been critical of proposals for the more extreme Chinese policies, particularly during the Great Leap Forward, but his criticism has been combined with complete loyalty in the execution of party policy once it has been agreed on. He is an able negotiator – cautious, persistent, and urbane – and his speciality has been foreign affairs.

Chou was born into a Kiangsu upper-class family with official connexions. He attended Nankai University, Tienstin, and was imprisoned after he took part in the student demonstrations of 4 May 1919. He studied in Japan, Paris, and Germany, and paid a short visit to Britain. During the period of co-opera-tion between the later Nationalists and the Communists in the KMT, Chou became head of the political department of Whampoa Military Academy (whose Director was Chiang Kai-shek), and he organized a successful strike which opened Shanghai to Chiang in 1927. Chou was later identified within the Communist Party with the Li Li-san line of continued strikes and armed risings, but successfully confessed his errors and went to Kiangsi to join Mao in 1931. He was Political Commissar to Chu Teh during the Long March. In the civil war Chou took a leading part in negotiations with the KMT, and is credited with the decision to release Chiang after the Sian agreement.

Since 1949 he has, during his constant travels, led Chinese delegations to the Geneva Conference over Vietnam, to the first Afro-Asian conference at Bandung, to the Soviet Union during the Hungarian crisis, and recently on tours gathering allies in Africa and Asia. His wife, Teng Ying-chao, is also a member of the CCP Central Committee, and an important political figure in her own right.

CHU TEH, b. 1886. The grandfather figure of the Chinese Communist state – conciliatory, portly, and benign. Chu Teh is the oldest of the major Communist Party leaders, and takes a less active part in state affairs than he did. He is, however, still the Vice-Chairman of the CCP Central Committee, and Chairman of the standing Committee of the National People's Congress.

Chu Teh was born in Szechuan into a rich peasant family. In the first half of his life he himself became a rich, corrupt, and many-wived warlord according to the conventional pattern. After he had reformed he went to Europe in 1922, where he became a member of the CCP, and then studied in Moscow. He joined Mao in Kiangsi in 1928. He was the main Chinese army leader through-out the Chinese civil war. Since 1949 Chu Teh has encouraged the army to accept party civilian control; and he has taken a particularly prominent part in

Politbureau discussions on agriculture and foreign policy. He has also led important Chinese delegations abroad.

CONFUCIUS (551–479 B.C.) (Kung Fu-tzu). The most famous man in China's history. His precepts dominated Chinese education and government for over 2000 years. Much to his disappointment he himself never held important political office, and the major part of his life was spent teaching disciples.

DALAI LAMA DANTZEN JALTSO, b. 1935. The Tibetan ruler in exile. Recognized as 14th reincarnation of the Dalai Lama in 1938. He attempted to work with the Chinese, in the interests of his people, after the conquest of Tibet, but fled to India in 1959. In a press interview he later accused the Chinese of starting 'a reign of terror' in Tibet.

HUNG HSIU-CHUAN (1814–64). The Heavenly King, the leader of the Taiping rebellion against the Ching dynasty. He claimed to be a Christian, Christ's younger brother, who had been called by God to rule China. In the 14 years of the rebellion he conquered much of South and Central China.

HUNG WU (1328–98). Founder of the Ming dynasty. The son of a poor peasant family, Hung Wu defeated the last servants of the Yüan (Mongol) dynasty, and re-established a Chinese state with a legal code and administrative system based on that of the T'angs.

KANG YU-WEI (1858–1927). Confucian scholar. Leader of the reform movement of 1898. Blamed Chinese weakness on misinterpretation of Confucianism. Remained loyal to the idea of limited monarchy, dismissed as reactionary by younger generation of the 1920s.

KAO KANG (d. 1955). Leader of pre-Long March revolution in northwest China. After 1949 he was Vice-Chairman of Central People's government, Chairman of the State Planning Commission, and Chairman of Northeastern People's Government. Committed suicide in prison 1955. Reason for fall not yet known. Possibly plotted independence of Manchuria, with or without connivance of the Soviet Union.

KUBLAI KHAN (1215–94). The grandson of Genghis Khan, and the founder of the Yüan dynasty in China. While Kublai made China part of the vast

Mongol empire, he did not interfere with basic Chinese social or economic institutions, or alter the content of traditional Chinese education.

KUO MO-JO, b. 1891. President of the Chinese Academy of Science, and Chairman of the All-China Federation of Literary and Art Circles. Kuo has been the leading government spokesman in dealing with the Chinese intellectuals and the various peace movements abroad. Before his complete absorption in politics, Kuo wrote poems, plays, and novels and did outstanding research on China's Bronze Age.

LAO-TZU (c. 600 B.C.). The probably mythical founder of Taoism. He is said to have advised Confucius, compiled the Book of the Tao, and departed westwards to India where he converted Buddha. The book attributed to him was probably compiled by several authors, not earlier than the 4th century B.C.

LI FU-CHUN, b. 1901. Chairman of State Planning Commission, Vice-Premier, member of CCP Politbureau, Central Committee and Secretariat. Economic specialist. Gained in influence from his support of Great Leap Forward policies.

LI LI-SAN, b. 1896. Studied in France. Became Secretary of Central Committee of the Communist Party in late 1920s. Criticized for 'blind actionism' (e.g. promotion of strikes and open revolt in towns – the course of action opposed by Mao). Since returning from Soviet Union in 1946, he has held minor government offices.

LIN PIAO, MARSHAL, b. 1908. A veteran of the southern soviets and the Long March. Became Minister of Defence 1959, is at present Vice-Chairman of the Politbureau and the Central Committee of the Party. He has recently taken an increasingly prominent part in national and international receptions and delegations; and his portrait is displayed in public places together with those of the other top leaders. (Mao, Liu, Chou, Chu Teh, Chen Yun, and Teng Hsia-ping.)

LI PO (701–62). Considered by many critics to be the greatest of China's poets. Despite his frequent drunkenness he was a favourite of the T'ang Ming Huang Emperor, but quarrelled with the emperor's favourite concubine. He was drowned when he fell from a boat trying to kiss the reflection of the moonlight.

Li Ssu (c. 280–208 B.C.). The prime minister of Ch'in Shih-Huang-ti; a Legalist; and held responsible for many of the ruthless and totalitarian innova-tions of the Ch'in emperor. Under Ch'in Shih-Huang-ti's successor Li Ssu was involved in a court intrigue and executed.

Li Ta-chao (1888–1927). One of the founders of CCP. As President of Peking University and Chief Librarian, organized study cells there in 1920. Executed for opposing militaristic ambitions of northern warlords.

Liu Pang (248–195 B.C.). Posthumously known as Kao-tsu. Founder of the Han dynasty. Reigned from 202 to 195 B.C. The son of a peasant who became a bandit chief, Liu Pang unified China after centuries of civil strife.

Liu Shao-chi, b. 1898. Since he succeeded Mao as Chairman of the Republic in April 1959, Liu has been recognized as Mao's most likely successor as general leader of the country. His previous importance had been particularly as a theorist, and as a party organizer.

Like Mao, Liu is a Honanese, partly educated at Changsha Normal School. As a young man he studied in Moscow. He joined the CCP in the year of its foundation, 1921, became a specialist in labour organization, and joined Mao in Kiangsi in 1932. He took part in the Long March, and thereafter he was largely concerned with party organization underground in KMT and Japanese-controlled China, and Party training in Yenan. Many of his pamphlets and speeches, like Mao's, have become communist classics, studied throughout today's China. The most famous, *How to be a good Communist*, was delivered to the Party training school in Yenan.

Since 1949 Liu has taken a prominent part in all major political decisions, particularly over state and party administration and over negotiations with the Soviet Union and other foreign communist countries. He is thought to have urged some of the more extreme measures of the Great Leap Forward, and to take a generally leftist view of Chinese policies.

Lu Hsun (1881–1936). Author. In spite of his opposition to materialism and to authoritarianism, Lu Hsun has been posthumously adopted by the commu-nists as the great exemplar of a socialist-realist writer. His most famous work is *The True Story of Ah Q*. It is a satire on the old order of Chinese life and a classic portrayal of national psychology.

219

Lu Ting-yi, b. 1907. Born into a Kiangsu landowning family. China's propaganda chief, also alternate member of Politbureau, a vice-premier, and Minister of Culture, Lu was prominent in the post-Hundred Flowers Movement and later Communist Party Rectification Campaigns.

Ma Yin-chu, b. 1882. Chinese economic theorist of international standing. President of Peking University 1951 to 1960. During 1958-9 Ma defended himself publicly against newspaper attacks alleging that he was a neo-Malthusian (connecting poverty with population growth), supported Keynesian economic theories, and denied the need for a class struggle in China.

Mao Tse-tung, b. 1893. The accepted leader of the CCP since 1935; but not a dictator according to the Stalinist pattern. Mao has consistently asked for and apparently considered advice from other Chinese leaders. Top level personal relations seem to be good, and Mao's influence is believed to be against vendettas of a defeated side or of the advocate, within the party, of a defeated policy. He is also believed to dislike unnecessary bloodshed.

Mao was Chairman of the Republic of China from 1949 until he resigned in 1959, in order, it was officially said, to devote more time to theoretical work. His prestige and popularity appear to be undiminished, and he continues to be Chairman of the CCP's Central Committee and of the Politbureau. His books and published speeches are required reading for all Chinese students of politics; and in China are given equal authority with the communist classics of Marx, Engels, and Lenin.

Mao was born into a prosperous Hunan peasant family. His father sent him to school to learn to do the family accounts; but Mao insisted on continuing his education to a modern school and then to college in Changsha, the provincial capital. Several of Mao's fellow-students became leaders in the Kuomintang or Communist parties. Mao himself found work in the library of the National University at Peking, where he met some of the leaders of the New Tide movement. In the collapse of the old imperial institutions the New Tide men stressed China's need for a new birth, based on Western knowledge. The study groups they formed provided much of the theoretical background for both the Nationalists and the communists.

In 1921 Mao was one of the delegates who founded the CCP. He organized the Autumn Harvest Rising in Hunan in 1927; and, after its failure, fled to the mountain stronghold of Chingkangshan. From there Mao organized a Chinese soviet on the borders of Kiangsi, Fukien, and Kwangsi provinces. He urged communist reliance on peasant support and guerrilla warfare rather than on open revolts in towns; and during the late 1920s and early 1930s, as the town revolts failed and their leaders were hunted down, Mao's views were accepted. In 1934 Mao led the Long March from the southern soviet to Yenan in North China. On the March, at a party conference at Tsunyi, Mao's leadership of the Party was confirmed. Thereafter Mao's public history has been the history of the Chinese Communist Party, and after 1949 of the Republic of China.

MAO TUN, b. 1896. Chinese novelist, playwright, critic. Long association with communism. Former Minister of Culture. Vice-Chairman of All-China Federation of Literary and Arts Circles.

MARCO POLO (c. 1254–1324). The Venetian traveller who became Kublai Khan's friend and servant. His account of his travels was disbelieved by his contemporaries, but, although modern scholars have found it inaccurate in occasional details, it is, in the main, true.

MATTEO RICCI (1552–1610). Italian Jesuit missionary who (with his companion Michael Ruggieri) opened China to Christian evangelization. Ricci was allowed to settle in Peking, where he attracted converts among the Chinese intelligentsia and gained general respect by his tolerant attitude to Chinese customs and his personal erudition.

MEI LAN-FENG, b. 1893. China's most famous actor, specializes in women's parts in traditional Peking opera. First went on stage at the age of 13, his father and grandfather also being actors. Sometimes government spokesman on opera, drama, or general cultural policy.

MENCIUS (371–289 B.C.) (Meng Tzu). Confucius' most influential follower. Like his master he failed to hold important state office, and became a teacher. His particular contribution to Confucianism was his stress on practical reform and the natural goodness of human nature.

MING HUANG (684–712) (the Brilliant Emperor). His reign is the high point of T'ang prosperity and culture. Administrative abuses were corrected, and the emperor made an unsuccessful attempt at fiscal reform. Military expeditions were sent outside China, but their expense and their defeats helped provoke rebellion.

PENG CHEN, b. 1899, Shaensi. Ranks among top dozen leaders. Mayor of Peking, First Secretary of the Peking Party Committee, member of CCP's Politbureau, Secretariat and Central Committee. He also receives foreign delegations, and heads Chinese delegations abroad.

PENG TEH-HUAI, MARSHAL, b. 1905. China's leading soldier and Minister of Defence until his dismissal in 1959. His fall was probably due to his disagreement with the Great Leap Forward policies and the breach with the Soviet Union.

PU YI, HENRY, b. 1906. Ex-emperor of China. Succeeded 1908, abdicated 1912. Restored for seven days in 1917. Japanese puppet emperor of Manchukuo 1934–45. Imprisoned in China 1949 to 1959. Worked in botanical gardens, Peking, 1959–63. Now engaged on research for autobiography.

SUNG MAI-LING (Madame Chiang Kai-shek), b. 1901. Educated at Wellesley College, USA. Sister-in-law of Sun Yat-sen. Married Chiang Kai-shek in 1927. Politically active. Rallied support for Chiang abroad, particularly in tours of the United States of America.

SSU-MA CH'IEN (c. 145/135–90 B.C.). The earliest and most influential Chinese historian. Travelled widely as a young man, then spent most of life as courtier of Emperor Wu of the Han dynasty. His *Records of the Historian* (*Shih Chi*) cover 2000 years of Chinese and East Asian history from the earliest time.

SUN YAT-SEN (1866–1925). The leading figure in the Chinese revolution of 1911, and a hero of both the Nationalists and the communists. Educated mainly outside China, he drew much of his early backing from overseas Chinese communities. He was ousted from power in 1913, and never regained full control of North China.

SUNG CHING-LING, b. 1890. The widow of Sun Yat-sen, is also the sister-in-law of Chiang Kai-shek, and a vice-chairman of the Chinese People's Republic. She is chairman of the Sino-Soviet Friendship Association, and of several welfare organizations. She was born into a wealthy, Western-orientated, Shanghai business family. She was educated partly in the United States, and assisted her husband in the foundation of the KMT.

TAO CHU, b. 1907. The most prominent party leader in South China. Took office in the south immediately after 1949. Member of the CCP Central Committee and First Secretary of its central south bureau.

TENG HSIA/PING, b. 1904. Probably the most important of the younger CCP leaders. He has been Secretary/General of the CCP Central Committee since 1954, and since 1956 a member of the Politbureau Standing Committee. He is a deputy premier, and during Chou En/lai's tour of Africa in 1963 was acting premier. He has negotiated with Asian communist leaders visiting Peking, has been a member of recent key delegations sent to Moscow to put the Chinese view on world communism, and he led the delegation to the Soviet Union sent in 1965.

TING LING, b. 1907. Authoress of considerable reputation. First joined with the communists in Yenan. She was arrested in the 1958 purge of rightists, and has not reappeared in public life.

TSENG KUO/FAN (1811–72). Mainly responsible for the defeat of the Taiping rebellion. Thereafter he tried, without lasting success, to revive the Confucian virtues and institutions, and subordinate to them enough Western science to make China a powerful, independent nation.

TZU HSI (1835–1908). 'Old Buddha'. Virtual ruler of China as co/regent and regent from 1861 until her death. Ambitious and able but without the education or imagination to grasp the full weakness of China confronted by the Western imperialism, and the far/reaching reforms the country needed.

ULANFU, b. c. 1903. The Chairman of the Inner Mongolian Autonomous Regional government; and the only non/Chinese on the Central Committee of the CCP. He is also Chairman of the Nationalities Affairs Commission (concerned with the administration of the autonomous regions of non/Chinese peoples living inside China's boundaries).

WANG WEI (698–759). Scholar, poet, and painter. His landscapes mark the beginning of mystical nature painting with a strong literary background.

WU HOU (625–705) (The Empress Wu). The most infamous woman in Chinese history; but an able and forceful ruler of the T'ang Empire. She was a concubine of the Emperor Tai Tsung, dominated his successor, and after she bore him a son, obtained the rank of empress. In 690 she deposed her son and had herself enthroned as empress.

YUAN SHIH-KAI (1859–1916). A viceroy of the Empress Tzu Hsi. Became President of the Republic after 1911. In 1915 he had himself proclaimed as the new emperor; but he postponed his enthronement and surrendered his civil authority when the provinces revolted against him.

Index

Numbers in italic refer to illustrations

Orwell, George (*see* text note 33, p. 208)
Overseas Chinese (*see also* Southeast Asia), 22-4, 64, 182, 191-2, *85*

PA-CHIN (*see* text note 9, p. 205)
Painting, 21, 28-9, 140-3
Pakistan, 165, 184; military dictatorship of, by China, 193
Paranoia among top leaders, 118
Peking, Geological Institute, 121
Peking Man (*see* text note 1, p. 205), *3, 90*
Peking University, 78, 79, 121
Peng Chen (*see* Who's Who, p. 222)
Peng Teh-huai, Marshal (*see* Who's Who, p. 222), 118-19
People's Consultative Conference (1949), 99
People's Courts, 103
People's Daily, 108, 117, 122, 188
Poetry, 28, 144-6 (*see* text note 33, p. 208), *77*
Poland, 183
Population, main centres of, 19, 155; numbers, 33, 165; pressures, 51-3, 165-7
Polo, Marco (*see* Who's Who, p. 221), 20
Postal service, 50, 59 (*see* text note 21, p. 206)
Pottery (*see* Ceramics)
Printing, invention of, 54
Prison conditions, 110 (*see* text note 30, p. 207), *68*
Prostitution, 75, 80, 100-1
Protest, duty of, 37, 133
Pu Yi, Henry (*see* Who's Who, p. 222)

QUEMOY ISLAND, 183

RATIONING, 159-60
Red Flag, 136
Red Star Over China (*see* Snow, Edgar)
Report of an Investigation into the Peasant Movement in Hunan, 80
Report on the Work of the Government, 162

Revisionism, 112, 187, 188 (*see* text note 50, p. 211)
Rhubarb trade, 55
Ricci, Matteo (*see* Who's Who, p. 221), *23, 24*
Roman Empire, 21-2 (*see* text note 7, p. 205)
Rousseau, J. J., 25-6
Royal Society delegation to China, 139
Rumania, 187
Russell, Bertrand, 78
Russia (*see also* Ili crisis and Soviet Union), 64

SALARIES IN CHINA, 135, 153, 156
San Men dam, 162
Science, Chinese (*see also* Atomic bomb and particular sciences), 54-5, 133-4, 138-9
Secret societies, 30, 101
Self-criticism, 109-10, 111-12
Settlement of China, 13-15, 16-19, 20-2
Shang dynasty, 13, 14, 15, 49, *5*
Shang, the Lord, 16
Shanghai (*see also* Population, main centres of; and Opera), 58, 97, 100, 101, 107, 108, 114, 117, 141, 152, 153, *32*
Shanghai coup, 73
Shantung, 21, 29
Shen Nung, 13
Shensi soviet (*see also* Yenan), 81, 82-5
Shimonoseki, Treaty of, 54, 58
Ships, 22
Sian Incident, 83-4
Silk, discovery (legendary), 13; manufacture, 37, *36*; trade, 21-2, 54
Sinkiang, 23, 115, 185, 187, 194
Sino-Indian border dispute, 193
Slogans, use of, 105-7, 133, 166
Snow, Edgar, 177, 178 (*see* text note 40, p. 209)
Social mobility (*see also* Class), 36 (*see* text notes 12, 13, 14, p. 206)
Social realism, 141, 143, 146
Songs of the Red Flag, 145

Wang Wei (*see* Who's Who, p. 223)
Wei period, 29
The White-haired Girl, 149
Women, position of, 30, 112–13, 156,
 165–7, 65, 66
Writing (Chinese), 13, 20
Wu Hou (*see* Who's Who, pp. 223–4)
Wu Tso-jen, 142

YANG SHIH, 16
Yangtze river and valley, 14, 18, 19, 20,
 87
Yellow River (*see* Hwang Ho)
Yellow Turbans, 119

Yenan (*see also* Shensi soviet), 86, 87, 98,
 99, 115, 177, 178, 182 (*see* text note 40,
 43, pp. 209, 210)
Yenan Forum (Resolution on art), 134–6,
 143, 145
Yonge, C. M., 146
Yu, Emperor, 14
Yüan dynasty (Mongol rule) (*see also*
 Kublai Khan), 49, 50, 119 (*see* text
 note 16, p. 206)
Yuan Shih-kai (*see* Who's Who, p. 224)
Yugoslavia, 187

ZAMBIA, 191